EVENING PRIMROSE

Discover the healing properties and beauty secrets of this natural oil

Kathryn Marsden

VERMILION
LONDON

Acknowledgements

My very grateful thanks go to the Wiltshire Library Service at Malmesbury, Trowbridge and Swindon for trawling the medical and scientific literature worldwide and supplying me with mountains of fascinating references relating to essential fatty acids and evening primrose oil.

This book is dedicated to Stephanie Goff

First published in 1993

1 3 5 7 9 10 8 6 4 2

Copyright © Kathryn Marsden 1993

The moral right of the Author has been asserted in accordance with the Copyright, Designs and Patents Act, 1988.

First published in the United Kingdom in 1993 by Vermilion an imprint of Ebury Press
Random House, 20 Vauxhall Bridge Road, London SW1V 2SA

Random House Australia (Pty) Limited
20 Alfred Street, Milsons Point, Sydney,
New South Wales 2061, Australia

Random House New Zealand Limited
18 Poland Road, Glenfield,
Auckland 10, New Zealand

Random House South Africa (Pty) Limited
PO Box 337, Bergvlei, South Africa

Random House UK Limited Reg. No. 954009

A CIP catalogue record for this book
is available from the British Library

ISBN 0-09-178039-X

The paper in this book is recycled

Typeset in Palatino by SX Composing Ltd, Rayleigh, Essex
Printed and bound in Great Britain by Mackays of Chatham PLC

This book gives non-specific, general advice and should not be relied on as a substitute for proper medical consultation. The author and publisher cannot accept responsibility for illness arising out of the failure to seek medical advice from a doctor.

Contents

Wayside weeds and miracle molecules

The golden elixir extracted from the seeds of the humble evening primrose plant has some astonishing medicinal properties.

It is a safe and efficacious natural medicine and has been recognized by Native Americans for hundreds of years for its value in treating skin disorders. Evening primrose oil was almost completely ignored by conventional science until early this century, but as serious research continues to prove the great value of this one-time wayside weed, medical misgivings have been giving way to respect and recognition.

Evening primrose oil – or more precisely, its active ingredient GLA (gamma linolenic acid) – is powerful yet gentle enough to deal with all kinds of conditions, from the simple to the severe. From acne to ageing, eczema to eyes, hormones to hangovers and pregnancy to prostate problems. You can use evening primrose oil to help overcome skin problems; achieve glossy hair and strong nails; keep colds and flu at bay; beat the pre-menstrual blues; and sail through the menopause.

The origins of evening primrose oil

The evening primrose plant is not a primrose at all but a member of the Onagraceae family and the genus *Oenotherae*, related to the rosebay willowherb and to the cultivated garden flowers clarkia and godetia. The 'primrose' part of the name relates to its stunning and delicately scented yellow flowers which open each summer evening from June to August.

A native of the Americas, some specimens of the plant were taken by collectors in the seventeenth century from Virginia to Europe and were catalogued by the famous botanist John Tradescant and the herbalist Nicholas Culpeper. But most strains crossed the Atlantic quite by accident in the soil which was used as ballast in the cargo ships that carried cotton to the Lancashire mills. To this day, the evening primrose is a familiar sight around the Liverpool docks and the sand dunes of the Fylde coast. It grows wild by road and railside, in disused stations, around derelict buildings and on waste ground; in fact, anywhere where it is able to flourish undisturbed. It's now becoming a familiar garden-settler, too.

Dozens of pods filled with tiny seeds are left behind after the yellow petals have fallen each day. It is these seeds which contain the golden oil that is the reason for the evening primrose's celebrity status. There are many medicines derived from plant extracts which are used to treat one or maybe two particular ailments. Evening primrose oil, however, has shown itself to be of exceptional therapeutic value in an amazing variety of illnesses.

Science began to take a serious interest in the plant at the end of the First World War when two German researchers, Heiduschka and Luft, became the first to carry out a proper analysis of the oil. They discovered that it contained something rather exceptional – a nutrient called GLA or gamma linolenic acid. GLA belongs to a group of vitamin-like substances known as essential fatty acids and it is GLA that is the valuable element in evening primrose oil.

It wasn't until the nineteen-sixties that more detailed studies were carried out by biochemist John Williams, who was responsible for bringing evening primrose oil and GLA research to public notice. Without his endeavours, the miraculous medical properties of the evening primrose might have remained unknown and the old 'wise' tales unproven.

The nineteen-seventies and eighties saw a surge in the number of clinical trials. Following promising work at Newcastle University, many sufferers of multiple sclerosis were advised to supplement their diets with evening primrose oil. Extensive long-term studies at the Universities of Bologna in Italy, Turku in Finland and the Department of Dermatology at Bristol Royal Infirmary, England, all proved that evening primrose oil was effective in the treatment of atopic eczema in adults and in children. Further trials have demonstrated its beneficial use for mastalgia (breast pain), pre-menstrual syndrome, viral infections, diabetic complications, high blood pressure, asthma, cystic fibrosis, hyperactivity, rheumatoid arthritis, heart disease and post viral fatigue. In my own practice, patients have reported such benefits as smoother skin, stronger nails, silkier hair, lowered cholesterol, less joint pain and improvements in osteo-arthritis, skin irritation, Raynaud's syndrome and vaginal dryness; ample evidence, if any were needed, that this remarkable oil certainly justifies its old nickname of 'king's cure-all'.

Scaremongers and sceptics

Not everyone is convinced, however. Even now, after so much positive and beneficial research, a few critics still believe that the claims for therapeutic uses of evening primrose oil are unproven, that there seems to be no nutritional need for it, or that most adults will get all the essential fatty acids they need from food. Despite scientific studies which suggest the exact opposite, a handful of commentators still feel that evening primrose oil should not be recommended for approved use on the basis that no one knows if taking large doses for a long period of time would have ill effects. And yet, despite exhaustive research, I have not been able to find one single report of any adverse effect caused by evening primrose oil either from short- or long-term use!

It is easy to put these brickbats into immediate perspective. Just compare them to the figures for hospital admissions caused by orthodox medical drugs – which are supposed to have undergone detailed and elaborate double-blind controlled trials. Ten thousand hospital beds are occupied each day by patients suffering from adverse drug reactions; not overdoses or addictions – just ordinary prescriptions. And the number of deaths per annum caused by misprescribing (by qualified doctors) could be as many as 15,000! That's three times as many lives as are lost on the roads each year! So much for 'approved use'.

Clinical studies using essential fatty acids continue to be conducted in laboratories, hospitals and universities throughout the world and the fund of knowledge about the many therapeutic uses of evening primrose oil is being updated constantly. But I can understand why the disbelievers are suspicious. How is it that one extraordinary ingredient appears to be so helpful to such a wide variety of different conditions as well as to so many people?

How evening primrose oil works

Essential fatty acids are just what their name implies – *essential*! They must be provided by the diet and cannot be made within the body. Don't be put off by the term 'fatty'; just think of them as essential nutrients like vitamins and minerals.

There are two 'families' of essential fatty acids: one type comes from linoleic acid and the other from alpha-linolenic acid.

Essential fatty acids form part of every single cell membrane and are involved in almost every biological function. Without the support, strength and flexibility they give to all cell membranes, skin would sag and age very rapidly, nails would flake and break and hair would be dull and dry. But to be of any value, essential fatty acids have to be converted into other fatty acids (such as the GLA which is also found in evening primrose oil, and, finally, into active components called prostaglandins before they can be put to work. Prostaglandins are balancing, regulating substances which behave rather like 'on-off' switches, communicating between cells and, second-by-second, either stimulating or inhibiting particular activities. Their discovery, in the nineteen-thirties, is usually credited to the Swedish scientist Dr Ulf von Euler, who found from his experiments that they reduced blood pressure. At that time, the previously unknown material was found in high concentrations in the prostate gland, hence the name 'prostaglandin'. Subsequent technical advances in research have identified thirty-six prostaglandins, active in every part of the body.

There are three main kinds of prostaglandins. Some are very beneficial and others (in excess) not so desirable. Their behaviour – and ultimate effectiveness – is determined by one particularly important factor: the kind of fat or oil they were made from.

The prostaglandins called Series 1 dampen down inflammation and are produced from the linoleic acid family found in certain foods of plant origin. Series 2 supports the inflammatory processes of the body (swollen glands, allergic responses, breast tenderness, joint swelling and so on. The body needs Series 2 prostaglandins but, in excess, they can be real troublemakers. Meat, milk, and related products are also direct sources of Series 2 prostaglandins. Series 3 prostaglandins come from foods such as oily fish and linseed (flax), sources of alpha-linolenic acid. The average Western diet usually contains too much of the aggravating Series 2 prostaglandins and not enough of the calming ones and threes.

Miracle molecules

This book is essentially about Series 1 prostaglandins – which could be called miracle molecules since they have so many terrific talents. Here are just a few of their abilities:

- Lowering cholesterol
- Preventing blood from becoming too sticky
- Relieving inflammation
- Balancing blood glucose
- Reducing blood pressure
- Fortifying the immune system and reducing the recurrence of viruses and other infections
- Regulating hormone activity
- Providing support to other nutrients
- Feeding the skin, hair and nails
- Healing wounds

Making GLA

The miracle molecules of series 1 prostaglandin depend on the body's ability to convert linoleic acid available in certain foods to GLA (gamma linolenic acid). In addition to a straightforward deficiency of linoleic acid, this conversion process is easily foiled or frustrated by a number of obstacles: excessive stress; ageing; viral infections; blood-sugar disorders; exposure to pollution; smoking, or radiation; deficiencies of some vitamins and minerals (especially vitamins A, C, E and B_6, biotin, magnesium, zinc, copper, and selenium); too much alcohol; or even by an excess of dietary fibre. In some conditions (eczema, for example), scientists believe there may be an inherent inability to convert essential fatty acids from one step in the metabolic pathway to another because the enzyme needed for the conversion (called delta-6-desaturase) is missing from the body.

Over-indulgence in not-so-healthy fat-laden goodies – especially saturated and processed fats – will result in too many of the not-so-helpful prostaglandins which wreak all kinds of havoc on the system, such as inflammation and clogged arteries. A particular hazard is something called a trans-fatty acid which turns up in many of the manufactured foods so common to the Western diet; a kind of 'Mr Hyde' to the cis-fatty acid's 'Dr Jekyll'. The cis form is healthy and biologically active but can, unfortunately, change into the unstable and positively dangerous trans type if exposed to factors such as heat, light, radiation and processing methods such as hydrogenation.

Once made, prostaglandins survive only for an instant, usually just long enough to carry out a particular task – and so, even when they are available, the essential fatty acids like GLA needed to make valuable prostaglandins are used up quickly and constantly. Getting enough GLA into the body is fraught with obstacles, which is why so many of us seem to be either deficient in certain essential fatty acids or have a higher than average requirement for them. Few people are likely to avoid stress, viruses, pollution and radiation all the time, and to eat the perfect diet. In addition, there is the possibility that large numbers of the population may no longer be able to manufacture enough of their own essential fatty acids because they lack a single vital enzyme.

Essential fatty acid deficiency doesn't happen overnight. It may exist for a long time before any symptoms are noticed and, if overlooked, misdiagnosed or ignored, could very well lead to one or more chronic conditions.

The GLA shortcut

Because evening primrose oil contains ready-made GLA it short-circuits the risky process of relying on the body to manufacture enough of this vital substance on its own. Keeping the body topped up with GLA in supplement form overcomes the easily triggered 'blocking' mechanism to ensure a permanent provision of Series 1 prostaglandins to protect tissues and cells.

Unfortunately, however, a great deal of myth and misinformation abounds about supplements. People are confused about if and when they should take evening primrose oil. Will it help their condition? How much should they swallow and for how long? Does it really make skin smoother? Is it true that it helps hangovers? How quickly does it work? I hope this book will clear up any confusion you may have and, most importantly, put you on the road to glowing good health.

Sources:

Schalin-Karrila M., Mattila L., Jansen C. T. & Uotila P., 'Evening primrose oil in the treatment of atopic eczema: effect on clinical status, plasma phospholipid fatty acids and circulating prostaglandins', *British Journal of Dermatology* 117 (1987), 11–19.

Biagi P. L., Bordoni A., Masi M., Ricci G., Fanelli C., Patrizi A. & Ceccolini E., 'A long-term study on the use of evening primrose oil in atopic children', *Drugs Exptl,Clin.Res.* XIV(4) (1988), 285–90.

Manku M. S., Horrobin D. F., Morse N. L. Wright S. & Burton J. L., 'Essential fatty acids in the plasma phospholipids of patients with atopic eczema', *British Journal of Dermatology* 110 (1984), 643–48.

Ziboh, V. A., & Chapkin R. S., 'Metabolism and function of skin lipids', *Prog.Lipid Res.* 27 (1988), 81–105.

Burton J. L., 'Dietary fatty acids and inflammatory skin disease', *The Lancet* (7 January 1989), 27–30.

Colbin, A., *Food & Healing* (Ballantine Books, 1986), 15–19.

Hill W., 'Essential fatty acids and rheumatoid arthritis', *Blackmores Communicator* 6(VI) (1987), 2–3.

Mansel R. E., Pye J. K., & Hughes L. E., 'Effects of essential fatty acids on cyclical mastalgia and noncyclical breast disorders. Omega 6 essential fatty acids', *Pathophysiology and Roles in Clinical Medicine* (1990), 557–66.

Mansel R. E., Harrison B. J., Melhuish J., Sheridan W., Pye J. K., Pritchard G., Maddox P. R., Webster D. J. T., & Hughes L. E., 'Effects of essential fatty acids on recurrent breast cysts. Omega 6 essential fatty acids', *Pathophysiology and Roles in Clinical Medicine* (1990), 567–73.

2

Beat the blues

Pre-menstrual syndrome (PMS) – is synonymous with irritability, anxiety, sudden mood swings, fatigue, tearfulness, temper tantrums, fluid retention, breast soreness and swelling, acne flare-ups and uncontrollable cravings. Vertigo, dizziness, restless limbs, overactive thoughts, lethargy, constipation, cramps, poor co-ordination (dropping and bumping into things) and excessive perspiration (particularly at night) are also characteristic of the condition. Varying estimates suggest that there may be between 150 and 300 symptoms associated with the syndrome. Women aged twenty-five to forty-five are the most likely to be affected from anything between three and fourteen days before the onset of a period.

According to Dr Guy Abraham, former Professor of Obstetrics and Gynaecology at the University of California Los Angeles, there may be more than one kind of PMS – he suggests as many as four main groups:

PMS-A for Anxiety

Disturbed sleep
Irritability
Nervous tension
Swings of mood
Palpitations
Panic attacks

PMS-C for Cravings

Dizziness
Fainting
Fatigue
Headaches/migraine
Palpitations
Increased appetite

PMS-D for Depression

Tearfulness
Confusion
Poor co-ordination
Forgetfulness
Loss of perspective

PMS-H for Hyperhydration

Fluid retention
Breast pain and tenderness
Abdominal bloating
Swelling of ankles
Weight gain

Whilst women are likely to have one or more symptoms from more than one group, these divisions provide useful guidelines. And they show that you are not alone, weird or abnormal just because your symptoms are different from someone else's.

The monthly blues – that dreaded depression – can make life seem insufferable to you (and you insufferable to others) until your period starts and the moribund mood melts away. I was told recently of a woman who, during her pre-menstrual week, was driving a friend to the local supermarket. 'Her voice got on my nerves,' she said, 'so I stopped the car and told her to get out. I just drove away and left her standing there.' From being a loved and respected 'rock of Gibraltar' for the rest of the month, this unhappy lady turned into an unreasonable and irritable grouch who took it out on everyone else around her. But such unwarranted behaviour, awful though it may have appeared, was simply not her fault.

The number of symptoms and their degree of intensity will vary from one individual to another but, however mild or severe, PMS should not be dismissed lightly – especially by those who have no comprehension of how terrible it can be. PMS isn't just miserable; it's a much-misunderstood millstone which, at best, limits your activities and, at worst, becomes a serious handicap. Jobs can be jeopardized, promotions passed by and relationships put at risk. The statistics for accidents, suicide attempts and crimes committed by women are all higher during this vulnerable time. For a few days each month, life can be a bitch!

Trish is thirty-two and had suffered with many of the typical PMS symptoms since she was fifteen. They grew worse during her twenties until they reached what she described as the 'glass-breaking, man-murdering' intensity. 'During the ten days before my period,' Trish says , 'I hated everyone, including my lovely husband and two children. I wanted to break things and scream. I cried all the time, too. The depression was absolutely awful.'

Trish also experienced acne flare-ups and cravings for chocolate which, she is convinced, made the skin problems worse. Her doctor suggested that she try evening primrose oil and a multivitamin for a few months to see if they would reduce the symptoms. 'The results were pretty astonishing,' she says. 'After four months I'm a calm, reasonable human being again.' Unexpectedly, Trish's craving for sweet foods has also gone. 'No bingeing on chocolate and no spots. It's wonderful. I'm certainly going to continue taking my evening primrose oil and vitamins for as long as I need to.'

Not 'all in the mind'

Trish knew that what ailed her was PMS, but some women are not even aware they are suffering with pre-menstrual syndrome; they are confused by their symptoms and don't understand that there is a reason for them. Irritability and mood changes are all too often seen as 'being female'. Indeed, until relatively recently, the 'time of the month' was the subject of satire and scorn. Genuine distress and despair were – and sometimes still are – misinterpreted as unreasonable neurotic behaviour. Thankfully, science has come to the rescue of the pre-menstrual female and proved beyond doubt that her ante-period mood is *not* 'all in the mind'. There are tangible, organic explanations for all that misery and torment. And with proof of its existence have come consideration, sympathy and new ways of coping with and curing PMS.

If you are unsure about the significance of PMS in your life, the chart on page 12 may be helpful. Using the letter codes, simply mark the days when symptoms are most troublesome. Once completed, it will be easy to see whether or not PMS is a problem.

Menstrual Chart

Indicate on the chart the days on which symptoms trouble you using the appropriate letter or letters from the key below.

Fill in months
(eg. May.)

Days of month.

	1	2	3	4	5	6	7	8	9	10	11	12	13	14	15	16	17	18	19	20	21	22	23	24	25	26	27	28	29	30	31
1st Month																															
2nd Month																															
3rd Month																															

Key to symptoms:

D depression. P pain – backache or headache. T tension or irritability. F fatigue. B bloated feeling. M menstruation.

A body out of balance

Although the actual reasons remain unclear, the villain of the pre-menstrual piece seems to be a disturbed pattern in the production of female hormones, which can be particularly out of kilter during the week before menstruation. Some studies point to an increase in oestrogen and to decreased progesterone in the days prior to a period. Others suggest not a lack of progesterone but an inability of progesterone receptors (found all over the body) to pick up and utilize that hormone. Further investigations blame other hormones such as aldosterone, prolactin and follicle-stimulating hormone (FSH). It seems that, between periods, female hormones ar involved in a kind of complicated juggling act, with the peak of this acrobatic activity occurring during the week before the next flow.

Most experts do agree that the 'anxiety' aspects of PMS are triggered by increased levels of oestrogen interacting with other hormones and enzymes. Noradrenalin, which can promote irritability and hostility, and excess serotonin, which can affect fluid balance, mood and concentration are also involved. Other balancing brain chemicals which would normally enhance relaxation and mental stability are (wouldn't you just know it!) in short supply at this time.

The over-simplified explanation that 'women are made that way', or that we are designed by nature to be intellectually and emotionally unstable is, of course, ridiculous nonsense and fails completely to explain why some women suffer so severely with hormonal disturbance, others only mildly, and some not at all.

Drug therapy

Progesterone and, in some cases, oestrogen, have been common prescription hormones for the treatment of PMS, given as tablets, capsules, pessaries, suppositories, or sometimes by injection. Unfortunately, some patients have reported side-effects such as increased blood pressure, nervous disorders, dizziness, depression, headaches, fatigue and (guess what?) PMS! What is the point in taking a drug which could cause the very symptoms you are trying to overcome? In the United States, manufacturers of progesterone drugs are required by law to place warnings in bold type in the *Physician's Desk Reference*, alerting doctors to an increased risk of birth defects. In addition, oestrogen drugs have been linked to an increased risk of cancer.

How evening primrose oil can help

Whilst experts disagree on the precise causes of PMS, many of the symptoms are those of essential fatty acid deficiency – a lack of those helpful prostaglandins described in chapter 1. Over the past few years, I have studied with great interest the use of evening primrose oil (and the few other GLA supplements, such as borage oil) in the treatment of pre-menstrual syndrome. I have been happy to recommend GLA to patients as a treatment and have witnessed some remarkable results. The beneficial changes have been particularly pleasing given that most of these (by now desperate) women had previously experienced a high incidence of failure with other kinds of treatment.

In most cases, evening primrose oil supplementation has been accompanied by a change of diet and, in relevant situations, by a vitamin B complex, multivitamin and/or multimineral. These additional suggestions appear to enhance the beneficial effects of the GLA.

Despite some reports which recommend taking supplements only during certain weeks of the cycle, my own experience in practice has been that patients benefit far more by taking multivitamins and GLA every day throughout the month.

Brenda was referred to me in July 1991. She was thirty-four and had lived with PMS since her mid-teens. 'Only, the older I get, the harder it is to cope with,' she confided.

'The worst things are the breast pain and the temper. I seem to flare up at everyone – and for no reason. And I can hardly bear to move around because my breasts hurt so much.' Brenda also experienced patches of sudden fatigue where 'I just have to go to bed and sleep, sometimes in the middle of the day . . . I run out of steam so quickly in the week before my period, it's almost as if I have no energy at all.'

I admired Brenda's honesty in telling me that her diet 'is terrible, especially pre-period' and 'I just can't leave chocolate alone and I pick at things between meals; all the wrong things, too'. She was happy to try any dietary changes but was worried about 'not sticking to it because of the cravings'.

I had no hesitation in recommending to Brenda that she try evening primrose oil together with some changes to her diet. But I did warn her not to expect any overnight miracles. Research suggests that deficiencies of essential fatty acids are extremely common, and that they build up over long periods of time before symptoms become apparent. Replacing those special nutrients can therefore take time. I pointed out to Brenda that it could be as long as twelve to sixteen weeks before the evening primrose oil made any difference, and that she must persevere with regular doses if she was to achieve any lasting benefits.

I see many new patients who tell me that they have already tried evening primrose oil but that it didn't work. On further questioning, I often find that they took one capsule per day for a week or so and then stopped because they noticed no changes. I would not prescribe evening primrose oil for less than four months before making any decisions as to its value in treating any particular condition. This caution has paid off many times. When evening primrose oil has been reintroduced on this basis to someone who had tried it before but failed on a much lower dosage, results have been excellent.

Brenda's new eating plan cut out coffee, sugar, salt, chocolate, cola, prepackaged ready meals, sweet cakes, biscuits and gooey pastries. She also gave up what she calls her 'weekly burger and chip trip'. The dietary changes and supplement recommendations which I made to Brenda are detailed in the 'Action-plan for PMS' at the end of this chapter.

Many people are surprised at how enjoyable an anti-PMS diet can be. It is important for PMS sufferers to understand that it isn't a crime to eat between meals. If you feel hungry, don't put up with that awful hollow emptiness until the next meal time. Instead, snack on sunflower and pumpkin seeds (rich in essential fatty acids), dried fruit, unblanched almonds, natural liquorice or the occasional carob sweet treat (from the health food store).

I saw Brenda in consultation every two months during her treatment. By her third visit, she reported a definite improvement, with much less severe breast pain and less mood swings. Soon after that, Brenda considered her PMS to be no longer a problem. 'I know the diet has helped a lot,' she told me, but I really do believe that evening primrose saved my sanity.'

Does diet hold the answer?

If your body isn't receiving the right kind of nourishment, or your lifestyle is such that any essential fatty acids which are eaten are destroyed or blocked, then those positive prostaglandins (see Chapter 1) won't be produced. Some PMS sufferers have been helped by the addition of a mineral supplement to their regular daily dose of evening primrose oil, perhaps because of the fact that the cramping pains associated with ovulation and menstruation are believed to be connected to low mineral status.

A definite negative relationship had been discovered between the intake of sugar, sugary foods and chocolate and the intensity of PMS symptoms. One particular study carried out at the University of Oregon examined the diets of more than 850 women. Those with the most severe premenstrual problems had the highest intake of sweet foods.

So cutting down on these empty calories seems like good advice.

Hypolycaemia and PMS – the link with low blood sugar

Many sufferers of pre-menstrual cravings are all too familiar with the 'hypo', that debilitating drop in blood sugar which leaves them feeling dizzy, shivery, sweaty and spaced out if they miss a meal or don't go for their regular sugar fix. The craving for sweet things happens because the body knows that very low blood glucose is a danger to life. The erratic nature of pre-menstrual hormones increases the likelihood of hypoglycaemia swings and the desire for sugar (or salt or coffee or alcohol; they all have a similarly stimulating effect). The trouble is, the benefits of such fixes are short-lived, and very soon another craving is creeping up on you.

Hypoglycaemia (or low blood sugar disease) is a condition where the levels of glucose in the blood fluctuate erratically and fall way below normal levels. Once again, hormones are involved. When the body is running out of fuel and the blood glucose falls slightly as a result, a message from the brain will trigger the desire to eat. If hormones are behaving themselves and meals are regular and well-balanced, then levels of blood glucose will be sustained from one meal to the next.

But in PMS other hormones are already disturbed and disorganized. All hormones work closely together and one imbalance is likely to create another. Add to that a list of other triggers such as missed breakfasts, skipped lunches, vending machine addiction (too much coffee and tea!), sugary snacks and late-night refrigerator raids, and those glucose-governing glands will be put under even more strain.

Hypoglycaemia overburdens the adrenal system as it struggles to keep up with wildly fluctuating blood glucose levels. In the process, large quantities of nutrients are used up, depriving the rest of the body of the co-factors and enzymes it needs in order to function. The devastating result of this over-exertion is not just hypoglycaemia but also stress-induced adrenal exhaustion.

Positive stress is a useful asset to everyday living. It gives us ambition and determination, and encourages a sense of achievement. Negative stress, on the other hand, is exhausting and draining. The stress-response is part of an evolutionary mechanism providing the body with enough emergency energy to deal with sudden trauma (the 'fight or flight' syndrome) – yet another mechanism which is dependent upon the body's hormones. Persistent mental and emotional distress (so often caused by or the cause of pre-menstrual aggravation) will mean blood sugar tries to stay high. But it can't be sustained – especially if you're not looking after yourself properly.

Like PMS, diagnosis of hypoglycaemia has been hampered by the medical belief that it is a product of the imagination. As a result, many victims of misdiagnosis are labelled, entirely unreasonably, as having psychological problems. Both Brenda and Trish almost certainly experienced unpleasant low blood sugar symptoms pre-menstrually and found that, by dealing with the hypoglycaemia, they felt fitter and had more energy.

Whilst the body behaves best on a varied and nutrient-dense diet, the only fuel upon which the brain can function is glucose. Persistently low blood glucose causes a disruption of brain chemistry by starving the brain of its vital supply. The result? Mental and emotional aberration, loss of perspective, irritability, and irrational behaviour. To confuse matters, taking pure glucose by mouth is not the best way to increase the body's natural supply and will only result in even more erratic hormonal behaviour and an increase in hypoglycaemic attacks. Glucose tablets and drinks are sometimes used in emergencies by diabetics to raise blood sugar quickly and prevent the onset of coma but this is not a practice to be recommended. The only healthy way to keep 'hypos' at bay is to eat a wholefood diet which contains complex carbohydrates (they release their energy slowly into the system without disturbing or unbalancing the glucose-controlling hormones).

American nutritionist Dr Michael Lesser believes that the majority of symptoms diagnosed by psychiatrists as neuroses are, in fact, mixed-up brain transmissions caused by insufficient glucose. Since the symptoms of 'neurotic behaviour', hypoglycaemia and pre-menstrual syndrome are so similar, balancing blood sugar levels could be a major step towards cancelling those cravings, banishing the binge and putting paid to PMS for good.

These are some of the more common hypoglycaemic symptoms. See how similar they are to those of pre-menstrual syndrome:

Anxiety and panic
  attacks
Periods of black
  depression
Blurred vision and
  headaches
Confused thinking
Dizziness and fainting –
  particularly if without
  food for more than
  three hours
Uncontrolled fits of
  crying
Poor co-ordination
Insecurity and lost
  perspective

Palpitations
Extreme coldness
Night sweats
Excessive sweating
  during the day,
  particularly when
  hungry
A need for frequent
  meals
Excessive thirst
Drowsiness, especially
  in the middle of the
  afternoon
Outbursts of temper
Irritability

Action-plan for PMS

- Take a good quality multi-vitamin/mineral complex together with evening primrose oil every day (see Chapter 10 for dosage). Study after study has demonstrated that multiple nutrient deficiencies are associated with PMS, particularly vitamin A, Vitamin B_6, vitamin E, the minerals calcium and magnesium and, of course, those very important essential fatty acids.
- Cut down on coffee and reduce other sources of caffeine – particularly tea, chocolate, and cola. This is especially important during the week before your pre-menstrual symptoms usually show. Women who consume large amounts of caffeine are likely to experience more severe PMS problems.
- Cut down on sugary and sweet foods. Sugar intake is significantly higher in PMS sufferers.
- Avoid salt and salty snacks. NB: Processed, canned and packet foods are often high in salt. Salt is believed to exacerbate hypoglycaemic symptoms.
- Reduce your intake of cow's milk and cheese. The calcium they contain, if eaten in excess, may disturb levels of magnesium – a vital nutrient in the management of the body's hormones. Dairy product consumption is higher where PMS exists and, as explained in Chapter 4, too many saturated or processed fats in the diet can block production of the anti-inflammatory and helpful Series 1 prostaglandins. Some diets recommended specifically for PMS encourage high levels of protein – which are supposed to sustain the appetite and prevent bingeing. But increased protein can mean increased fat intake – usually the wrong kind – together with a greater risk of heart disease, kidney disorders and breast cancer.
- Ease up on sausages, bacon, burgers, meat pies and processed tinned meats. They can be high in saturates, too.

- Beware of margarines and spreads which are made with hydrogenated vegetable oils. these processed yellow fats can inhibit SEries 1 prostaglandins. (For more information, see Chapter 4.)
- Avoid 'diet' foods and drinks which contain artificial sweeteners. Investigations show that they can disturb blood glucose tolerance just as severely as ordinary sugar.
- Always have breakfast but avoid sugar-laden breakfast cereals. Check the labels for hidden sugar. Choose wholegrain muesli or porridge instead. If you really cannot face food first thing, then have something sustaining as soon as you can manage it.
- Whether you are at home, in the office or travelling around, plan ahead and don't go for more than three hours without food. Eat several small meals each day instead of one or two larger ones.
- Carry a snack with you. Instead of chocolate or crisps, try sunflower seeds, pumpkin seeds, unblanched almonds, mixed cereal bars or dried fruit.
- Don't wait until you are ravenous before you eat.
- Don't be a slave to low-calorie weight-loss diets. They will do nothing for your long-term health and can only make both your PMS and blood sugar problems worse.
- Have a light snack about an hour before bed. This helps to stabilize your blood sugar throughout the night and reduces the risk of night sweats.
- Make sure your diet contains plenty of:
  - Wholegrains such as brown rice, rye, millet, buckwheat, oats and barley. Enjoy wholewheat pasta, oat cakes, rice biscuits, rye crackers and jacket potatoes.
  - Fresh fish, free-range poultry and free-range eggs.
  - Bio-yoghurt and buttermilk.
  - All kinds of vegetables, vegetable soups, pulses, salads and fresh fruit. Aim for two or three pieces of fruit each day, a good-sized salad and two or three servings of fresh vegetables.
  - Nuts and seeds – excellent sources of fatty acids.
  - Instead of fruit squashes and carbonated drinks, have

diluted fruit juices, vegetable juices, grain-based coffee substitutes, herbal teas and mineral water.

○ Drink plenty of water each day – at least 4 glasses, preferably 6, between or before meals. For some people drinking more water helps to *reduce* the fluid retention associated with PMS.

● Share your concerns with family and friends. Those close to you are much more likely to understand and to comfort you if they are aware of your feelings and symptoms.

● Wear loose fitting, comfortable clothing on days when you feel irritable, 'scratchy' or bloated.

● Don't push yourself into tasks which require attention to detail if you are not feeling up to it. Leave them for days when you are feeling mentally and physically stronger.

● Take regular exercise. This doesn't mean a daily marathon or working-out to exhaustion. A twenty-minute brisk walk or a ten- or fifteen-minute session on a mini-trampoline (rebounder) is enough.

● Learn how to relax. Take time out for yourself and don't feel guilty about it. If you are not at your best, you can't do your best for others. No one should be on permanent duty. Take a break and pamper yourself. How about a regular massage, a facial, a deep and soothing bath? – or just curl up in a quiet corner with a favourite novel. Practise some deep-breathing exercises every day.

If none of these things works for you, or you are concerned in any other way about your health, please see your GP without further delay. PMS symptoms may be related to a low-grade infection of the pelvic organs or more serious pelvic inflammatory disease and can also be linked to either too much or too little thyroid hormone, poor bowel function or a sluggish liver. Ask for tests to be carried out – and for a second opinion if you are not happy with any diagnosis. An automatic and hurriedly written prescription for painkillers or antidepressants could be compared to papering over the cracks instead of investigating why the cracks appeared!

Sources:

Piesse J., 'Nutrition factors in the premenstrual syndrome', *International Clinical Nutrition Review* 4(2) (1984), 54–81.

Rossignol A. M. *et al.*, 'PMT and sugar', *J.Repro.Med.* 36(2) (1991), 131–6

Lonsdale D., 'Why premenstrual syndrome responds to nutritional therapy', *J.Adv.Med.* 3 (1990), 257–64.

McDonald R. H. *et al.*, 'Effects of dopamine in man: Augmentation of sodium excretion, glomerular filtration rate and renal plasma flow', *J.Clin.Invest.* 43 (1964), 1116.

Puolakka J. *et al.*, 'Biochemical and clinical effects of treating the premenstrual syndrome with prostaglandin precursors', *J.Repro.Med.* 30(3) (1985), 149–53.

Wright J., 'The glucose-insulin tolerance test and its relevance to essential hypertension and HDL/LDL cholesterol abnormalities', *International Clinical Nutrition Review* 10(3) (1990), 381–2.

Rossignol A. M., 'Caffeine-containing beverages and premenstrual syndrome in young women', *Am.J.Public Health* 75(11) (1985), 1335–7.

Horrobin D. F., 'The role of essential fatty acids and prostaglandins in the premenstrual syndrome', *J.Repro.Med.* 28(7) (1983), 465–8.

Taylor L., Rachman S., 'The effects of blood sugar level changes, on cognitive function, affective state and somatic symptoms, *J.Behav.Med.* 11 (1988), 279–91.

Gugliano D., Torella R., 'Prostaglandins E1 inhibits glucose-induced insulin secretion in man', *Prostaglandins Med.* 48 (1979), 302.

Abraham G. E., 'Nutritional factors in the etiology of premenstrual tension syndrome', *J.Repro.Med.* 28(7) (1983), 446–64.

Abraham G. E., 'Premenstrual tension', *Prob.Obstet.Gynecol.* 3(12) (1980), 1–39.

Brush M. G., 'Evening primrose oil in the treatment of premenstrual syndrome', reported in *Clinical Uses of Essential Fatty Acids* (Eden Press, Montreal, 1982), 155–162.

3

Staying young and beautiful

The menopause or 'change of life' used to be looked upon as the season when a woman retired gracefully from her child-bearing years and looked forward to a new cycle of life; a positive and enjoyable time with more freedom, fewer family restraints, no more monthly periods and no risk of unwanted pregnancy. It is an inevitable and natural occurrence – the gradual decrease of oestrogen production from the ovaries and the cessation of menstrual bleeding – which usually occurs between the ages of forty-seven and fifty-four. Unfortunately, nowadays the menopause is more likely to be dreaded and suffered than enjoyed. Unpleasant symptoms are said to affect nearly eighty per cent of women, half of them for up to five years, and twenty-five per cent suffer for as long as ten years! Publicity surrounding the menopause is full of negativity, far closer to its alternative name 'climacteric' (Greek for 'a step in the ladder'), which also means crisis.

Margaret is fifty-four. Three years ago, she began to suffer with mastalgia (breast pain), but assuming that it was a symptom of the menopause and that nothing could be done to help, she put up with the discomfort. She had other menopausal symptoms too, including night sweats, irritability, dizziness and vaginal dryness. When a friend told her that evening primrose oil had helped ease her own menopausal distress, Margaret decided to try it.

I usually discover this kind of information from patients in consultation, but in Margaret's case we met in the queue at the supermarket check-out and, because of the long wait, began chatting. Margaret said she would ring me in a few months' time to let me know how she was getting along.

It seems that, after nearly six months, she was on the verge of giving up her daily evening primrose oil capsules because she had decided that they probably weren't going to work. 'I intended to finish the pack I was taking but, before I did, the symptoms began to improve. After all that time, I began to feel better.' She told me she was enjoying the additional benefits of stronger nails, clearer skin and a happier sex life! The vaginal dryness which had plagued her since the start of the menopause 'improved immeasurably'.

Margaret wanted to know why the menopause can wreak such havoc and was particularly concerned about brittle bone disease. I explained that, as with PMS, unbalanced hormones are the perpetrators of a great deal of this trouble. Hormones are chemical 'couriers' secreted by a number of glands in the body which belong to the endocrine system. Their messages make lots of things happen such as raising or lowering blood sugar, stimulating gastric juices, regulating and marshalling metabolic rate and, of course, controlling fertility. But if they misbehave, it's easy to mistake the menopause for some kind of madness and deep depressive gloom; an emotional roller-coaster nightmare of being trapped and out of control.

The long list of symptoms is enough to make anyone feel down: hot flushes; cold sweats; intolerance of extreme temperatures; abdominal bloating; breast tenderness; dry skin; dry hair; dizziness; vertigo; depression; exhaustion; weight gain; headaches; fluid retention; palpitations; irritability; insomnia; vaginal dryness and reduced sexual activity; poor bladder control; and – the most publicized fear of all – osteoporosis, the condition which Margaret was so concerned about.

Paranoia over crumbling bones

The concerns and dangers of brittle bone disease are very real, with statistics just about as encouraging as those for the menopause itself. It is thought to affect thirty per cent of women over sixty and fifty per cent of those over seventy, causing crumbling vertebrae, loss of height, dowager's hump and frequent fractures. In the most severe cases a simple sneeze could break a rib!

The calcium in your skeletal structure is in a kind of perpetual motion, under the control of two hormones in particular. One of these, calcitonin, encourages the deposit of calcium to the bones and the other, parathyroid hormone, withdraws it. Oestrogen retards parathyroid hormone activity so that, if oestrogen is no longer being produced, the bones will lose more calcium than is being replaced.

Research has also come up with a link between thyroid hormone drugs and an increased risk of osteoporosis. Although the results of these studies are not conclusive, any woman who is taking regular medication for a thyroid condition should be monitored regularly by her GP to make sure she is not taking the drug in excess.

Natural compensation

The properly nourished body has a prearranged and very clever mechanism for keeping some all-important oestrogen in circulation. A gland in the brain, called the pituitary gland, sends a message to the adrenals to increase their own oestrogen output so that menopausal symptoms are overcome and certain sexual characteristics maintained. Where the endocrine system has suffered from over-stimulation especially due to stress, poor diet, lack of essential fatty acids and other nutrients, and hypoglycaemia, this back-up system fails to operate. So common is this failure that the severe physiological changes associated with the menopause have come to be accepted as the norm.

Hot flushes, cold sweats and difficulty in coping with marked temperature changes are common menopausal symptoms. Shattered adrenal function can frequently be related to these bothersome symptoms. Rest, relaxation, and removal of potential food allergens and unnecessary stimulants from the diet all go a long way to easing the strain and curbing the creeping hot flush.

It is an unfortunate fact of female life that those who have suffered with difficult periods, pre-menstrual symptoms or other hormonal imbalances are often at greater risk from menopausal misery than those who have an easier time of things. Sound nutrition and sensible supplementation can help enormously to restore the status quo.

HRT – panacea or perilous potion?

Margaret and I also talked about the pros and cons of hormone replacement therapy (HRT) which has been proclaimed widely as the answer to all menopausal ills. It certainly does seem to be a popular treatment for what has become the high-risk disease of osteoporosis, and has helped many women enjoy, rather than suffer, their menopausal years. A synthetic oestrogen drug was the first hormone replacement to be introduced in the sixties – welcomed as the 'forever feminine' antidote to ageing. However, when reports began to show a fivefold increase in the risk of cancer of the uterus, the popularity of this type of HRT declined. A new form of the treatment (with added progesterone) was then bought in, which appeared to reduce the danger. This combination is very effective at preventing osteoporosis; dwindling sex lives are reported to be revitalized, fatigue overcome and the quality of hair and skin said to improve. It is easy to become a push-over for HRT – and its benefits have been reported by some very famous faces. Who wouldn't be impressed?

But it isn't a question of simply taking a daily dose of hormones and expecting everything else to take care of itself. This kind of therapy does not suit everyone; nor is it without its side effects. Varying figures still quote an increase in the incidence of some cancers (the risk is said to double every six years), and other sources point to heart disease, stroke and arteriosclerosis. There is also concern about using a product whose long-term effects may not be known fully for several more years. In some people, even the short-term and limited use of HRT can upset significantly the internal balance of natural hormones.

Apart from any possible unknown dangers, the use of HRT does perpetuate the monthly bleed, a nuisance for some women who thought they had said goodbye to periods. And although there is no risk of pregnancy on hormone replacement therapy, users can still suffer with pre-menstrual type symptoms including irritability and breast tenderness.

Hormone replacement therapy

For	*Against*
Reduces the risk of osteoporosis	Increases risk of liver and gallbladder disease
When used without progesterone, decreases risk of heart disease	With progesterone, there may be an increase in stroke & heart disease
Added progesterone decreases incidence of uterine cancer	With progesterone, increased risk of breast cancer
Eliminates hot flushes	Greater likelihood of fibroids
Reduces vaginal dryness	Maintains menstrual cycle
	Oestrogen-only therapy may elevate suicide risk

Evening primrose oil and diet for the menopause

Natural hormones cannot be created in the first place without the support of nourishing food. And since there is a likely link between nutritional deficiency and menopausal maladies, it must make sense to protect against their onset or, if they pre-exist, to treat them with good nutrition and the sensible use of supplements.

The best protection against osteoporosis is to ensure optimum nutritional intake, not just during the early years of growth and up to peak bone mass around the age of thirty to thirty-five but also continuing into middle age and beyond. Worldwide population studies show that where this optimum is not maintained, osteoporosis risk is far greater.

The most abundant mineral in the human body, calcium (and the synergistic nutrients including GLA from evening primrose oil, which work with it), may hold one of the most important keys to osteoporosis prevention. The body excretes between 500 mg and 900 mg of calcium each day which needs to be replaced via the food we eat. In addition, calcium absorption decreases with age so that daily losses could be greater than the amounts which are supplied by many diets.

The official UK recommendations for average intake are 700 mg of calcium daily for the 19+ age group, but this is considered by many experts to be a long way short of the optimum level. Some authorities believe that amounts of 1000 mg to 1200 mg are closer to an ideal intake. Others say that lower levels of calcium are acceptable as long as the supporting nutrients are also available in sufficient amounts.

All vitamins, minerals and essential fatty acids (including those found in evening primrose oil and fish oil) function very closely together in a kind of interlinking chain. Taking extra calcium on its own without the support of other nutrients is unlikely to provide sufficient defence and could lead to severe imbalances of other minerals. But supplying the body with a sensible supplement programme coupled to a healthy diet has the exciting potential to reduce the appallingly high osteoporosis statistics and, at the same time, improve other menopausal symptoms.

Many essential nutrients rely on each other for support.

Calcium works in synergy with magnesium and both minerals play a vital role in producing and regulating hormones. Without magnesium, calcium cannot be absorbed, but if there is too much calcium, magnesium won't be utilized. And essential fatty acids are unlikely to function to full effect if magnesium or calcium are missing.

Action-plan for the menopause

• Try evening primrose oil (see Chapter 10 for dosage) and fish oil supplements. Without GLA and EPA, the supportive prostaglandins which figure in all hormonal activity cannot be manufactured. (Don't forget that prostaglandins are also needed to regulate calcium metabolism.) These nutrients have an established and enviable track record in the treatment of other hormone-related disorders such as endometriosis, difficult periods and pre-menstrual syndrome. Whilst evening primrose oil is not a hormone replacement, I believe it is helpful to those going through the menopause as well as offering additional support to those who are undergoing HRT.

• With your evening primrose oil, take a daily supplement of vitamin B complex (25 mg) and vitamin E (100 iu – 200 iu). They can help to make the evening primrose oil more effective. And don't forget that fish oil can help here too.

• Watch your intake of saturated fats. Cut down on fatty and deep-fried foods, pork, ham, bacon, pork pies, sausages, tinned and preserved meats, chocolate, milk, cakes, biscuits, pastries and hydrogenated spreads. Not only do excess saturates prevent prostaglandin production, they can also form insoluble soaps which prevent calcium uptake.

• But don't cut down too far on fat. Use cold-pressed oils for salad dressings. Cook with olive oil and don't be afraid to include small amounts of butter and additive-free cheese.

- Don't strive to be too thin. Women on a nourishing diet and with a bit of padding are likely to make more oestrogen. Underweight skinnies have a much greater risk of bone fractures.
- Reduce your intake of stimulants, i.e. salt, sugar, tea, coffee, cola and other sugary soft drinks, and alcohol. Substitute other fluids such as vegetable and fruit juices, grain-based coffee substitutes, fruit and herbal teas, and water.
- Drink a glass of water (about 250 ml, and preferably filtered) as soon as you wake up in the morning and drink more throughout the day – between or before meals.
- It is well-known that inactivity causes calcium to be lost from the bones so, if possible, take regular exercise. Some simple stretching and deep breathing exercises plus a fifteen-minute brisk walk every day should be enough.
- Let your skin see daylight and fresh air. Absorption of calcium relies upon there being adequate vitamin D in the body. A thirty-minute sunbathe is known to produce 300-350 units of this sunshine vitamin (don't overdo the sun, however). Even going outside on overcast winter days can be helpful.
- Don't let hypoglycaemia get the better of you (see Chapter 2).
- Eat little and often.
- Eat plenty of magnesium-rich foods, vital for the proper utilization of calcium and essential fatty acids. Good dietary sources are nuts, seeds, pulses, fish, lean meat, brown rice, whole rye, seafoods, bananas, dried fruit and green vegetables.
- Eat plenty of calcium-rich foods, too. Bio-yoghurt, canned fish, nuts, pulses, wholewheat flour, oatmeal, root vegetables, winter cabbage, watercress, oatmeal, maize, brown rice, blackstrap molasses, fresh fish, broccoli and kale all provide valuable amounts of calcium and are preferable to fat-laden dairy products.
- Don't rely on milk as a primary calcium source. The calcium from it is very poorly absorbed by large numbers

of the population and milk itself is a common allergen. It is also mucus-forming and is a known aggravator of catarrah and sinus problems.

- Nutrient-dense sources of protein foods are vital to good health but don't eat protein (in the form of meat, fish, cheese, eggs and milk) to excess. Too much can cause kidney damage and calcium loss. The officially recommended intake is 45 mg to 55 mg daily (1½–2 ounces).

- If your practitioner recommends mineral supplements, be extremely cautious about quality. Calcium is a particular case in point. A scan of the studies which have investigated calcium and osteoporosis reveals that poor-quality calcium carbonate did not show any beneficial effects while the more expensive and more easily absorbed calcium citrate malate increased bone density in post-menopausal women. Results of recent trials now indicate that bone mass can be rebuilt by taking a daily dose of calcium with a vitamin D supplement.

- Consider the use of *probiotic supplements*, especially if you have had antibiotics in any quantity over the previous year or so. Those will help you achieve the right balance of friendly gut flora which is essential, not only for assisting calcium absorption, but also for the efficient recycling of natural oestrogens in the body.

- Don't smoke, and avoid other people's cigarette pollution as much as possible.

- Don't drink alcohol to excess. However, there's no need to become teetotal. Studies show that a glass of wine a day is not only good for the blood but may have some protective effect against heart disease. A glass of red wine with a meal can aid digestion, too.

- Relax. Unhunch those shoulders, unclamp that clenched jaw. Breathe more deeply, moving your diaphragm and abdomen – not just the upper chest area. It's relaxing, improves circulation and helps to transport nutrients more efficiently around the system. For more information on stress, see Chapter 7.

- Don't underestimate the support of friends and family.

They are far more likely to understand and to help you through problem days if you explain your symptoms and feelings to those close to you.

- Dandelion coffee, raspberry leaf tea, blackberry leaf tea, natural liquorice, *dong quai* and *agnus castus* are also helpful in relieving menopausal symptoms.
- Get plenty of sleep.

Looking after yourself makes good sense at any age. Eating a nutrient-dense diet, taking regular exercise, learning how to rest and relax and taking the right nutritional supplements – all these things can help to make the menopausal years the beginning of an exciting, creative and fruitful time in a woman's life.

If menopausal symptoms don't improve on this programme, do visit your GP or practice nurse for a health check and ask your nutrition practitioner to check for candidiasis and food sensitivities.

Sources:

Hawkridge C., Brush M. G., 'Improvements in communication and nutrition in the support of endometriosis sufferers', in *Functional Disorders of the Menstrual Cycle*, (Wiley & Son, 1988).

Davies, Dr Stephen and Stewart, Dr Alan *Nutritional Medicine*, (Pan Books, 1987).

Mayes, Adrienne *Dictionary of Nutritional Health* (Thorsons, 1986).

Kung, A. W. C. *et al.*, 'Bone mineral density in premenstrual women receiving long-term physiological doses of levothyroxine', *Journal of the American Medical Association* 265 (1991), 2688–91.

Walker, R. M. & Linkswiler, H. M., 'Calcium retention in the adult human male as affected by protein intake', *Journal of Nutrition* 102 (1972), 1297–1302.

Harvey J. A., Zobitz M. M., Pak C. Y. C., 'Dose dependency of calcium absorption; a comparison of calcium carbonate and calcium citrate', *J. Bone Min.Res.* 3 (1988), 253–8.

Nicar M. J., Pak C. Y. C., 'Calcium bioavailability from calcium carbonate and calcium citrate', *J.Clin.Endocrin.Med.* 61 (1985), 391–3.

Schuette S., Knowles J., 'A comparison of calcium absorption from calcium citrate versus calcium H_2PO_{42} by two methods', *Am. J.Clin.Nutr.* 45 (1987), 863.

Dawson-Hughes B., Dallal G. E., Krall E. A. *et al.*, 'A controlled trial of the effect of calcium supplementation on bone density in post-menopausal women', *N.Eng.J.Med.* 323 (1990), 878–83.

Dawson-Hughes B. *et al.*, 'Effect of Vitamin D supplementation on wintertime and overall bone loss in healthy postmenopausal women', *Ann.Int.Med.* 115 (1991), 505–12.

Haddad J. G., 'Vitamin D – solar rays, the Milky Way, or both?', *N.Eng.J.Med.* 326 (1992), 1213–15.

Yeater R., Martin R., 'Senile osteoporosis: The effects of exercise', *Postgrad.Med.* 75 (1984), 147–9.

Lee C. J., Lawler G. S., Johnson G. H., 'Effects of supplementation of the diets with calcium and calcium-rich foods on bone density of elderly females with osteoporosis', *Am.J.Clin.Nut.* 34 (1981), 819–23.

Smith E. L., Gilligan C., Smith P. E., Sempos C. T., 'Calcium supplementation and bone loss in middle-aged women', *Am.J.Clin.Nut.* 50 (1989), 833–42.

Smith K. T., Heaney R. P., Flora L., Hinders S. M., 'Calcium absorption from a new calcium delivery system (calcium citrate malate)', *Calif.Tissue Int.* 41 (1987), 351–2.

Sheikh, M. S. *et al.*, 'Gastrointestinal absorption of calcium from milk and calcium salts', *New England Journal of Medicine* 317 (1987), 532–6.

Department of Health Dietary Reference Values for Food, Energy and Nutrients for the United Kingdom: Report of the Panel on Dietary Reference Values of the Committee on Medical Aspects of Food Policy, (HMSO, 1991).

Smith S., *et al.*, 'A preliminary report of the short-term effect of carbonated beverage consumption on calcium metabolism in normal women', *Arch.Int.Med.* 149 (1989), 2517–19.

Villar J., Repke J. T., 'Calcium supplementation during pregnancy may reduce preterm delivery in high-risk populations', *Am.J. Obstet.Gynecol.* 163 (1990), 1124–31.

West D., 'How junk food and pollution are hurting women's health; a baffling symptom mix', *Health News & Review* 7(5) (1989), 5.

4

Evening primrose oil, weight loss and diet

The innumerable benefits of evening primrose oil in the management of chronic illness continue to be researched and reported. As a direct result, a great many previously intractable conditions are responding positively to treatment whilst fresh studies keep on finding new talents and tasks for this able oil. One area in which I believe it may be of even more help than is at present realized is in improving the health of the dieter.

Twentieth century Western culture has, for some peculiar reason, inflicted upon us the idea that in order to be beautiful we must be thin. As a result, millions of women, in particular, spend inordinate amounts of time following low-fat and low-calorie weight-loss diets. As soon as one regime is finished and the lost weight has inevitably crept back, they begin another diet – and then another. The consequences of this yo-yo eating pattern can be devastating.

At my nutrition clinic, I am seeing increasing numbers of people who are suffering with what appear to be fat deficiency disorders. Their long-term devotion to fat-free diets has left them with increased joint stiffness, dry skin, reduced resistance to infections and, in the case of many women, vaginal dryness. The reintroduction of sensible amounts of good quality oil (such as extra-virgin olive oil) into the diet together with regular supplements of evening primrose oil is often enough to resolve these unpleasant problems without increasing bodyweight. A happy side effect of this treatment is that both olive oil and evening primrose oil are believed to be helpful in balancing blood cholesterol and could therefore be beneficial in reducing the risk of heart and other serious degenerative disease.

Mary was fifty-five when she first visited me. Well into the menopause, she had been on a low calorie weight-loss programme for most of her life. 'I always seem to be able to lose weight easily but it goes on so quickly,' Mary complained. 'Since I started the menopause, my skin is dry and very flaky and my arthritis, which has never been too much of a problem, is much worse. I'm hungry all the time, too.' More seriously, Mary had recently been diagnosed as having gallbladder problems caused, her doctor believed, by poor eating habits and yo-yo dieting. Her cholesterol and blood pressure were also on the high side.

Most dieters are undernourished

Mary's difficulties are, unfortunately, not uncommon. Depending upon body size and activity level, an adult needs anything between 1500 to 2000 kilocalories each day if he or she is to be properly nourished. But most diets allow a meagre 1000 or 1200 calories per day – not nearly enough to provide adequate energy. In addition, experts are concerned at the increased number of cases of gallstones and heart disease in people on quick fix weight-loss programmes.

Constant calorie-counting and cutting down on food intake inevitably reduces the number of nutrients available to the body for normal functioning, replacing and repairing worn-out cells, and protecting against damage. A significant shortcoming of crash dieting is its reliance upon processed, packaged food; reduced dietary fibre; and the lack of essential fatty acids and other nutrients.

I explained the principles of food-combining to Mary and suggested that by not mixing proteins and starches at the same meal and by eating fruit separately from other foods, she would be able to lose weight without reducing her calorie intake. I also recommended that she cut down on convenience foods and processed ready meals, even though they are supposed to be low in calories. I suggested that she change from polyunsaturates to monounsaturated extra-virgin olive oil for cooking and salad dressings and that she increase her intake of fresh salad foods, vegetables, seeds, oily fish and fresh fruit. I recommended daily capsules of evening primrose oil to help the dry skin and joint stiffness.

After three months, Mary reported a definite reduction in symptoms and a loss of just over a stone in weight! Her blood pressure and cholesterol were within normal limits and the gallbladder colic which she had found so delibitating had diminished significantly; in fact, there is now a chance that she may not need surgery.

But gallbladder and heart disease are only two in a long list of potentially serious health problems which can occur in this type of situation: menstrual and pre-menstrual disorders, menopausal distress, weakened immunity, dry skin, dull hair, palpitations, anxiety, depression, aching and twitchy limbs, joint stiffness, vaginal dryness and painful intercourse, fatigue and infertility are just some of the more familiar symptoms which can occur as a result of dangerously low fatty acid intake.

Another problem associated with inadequate supplies of calories and missed meals are those horrible and hollow hunger pangs. But when a craving creeps up on you, how often is it satisfied with a healthy salad, a handful of seeds and nuts or piece of fruit? No – it's sugary or fatty junk which is usually the order of the day.

Clearing up the confusion

When questioned, most people admit, even now, to being confused about cholesterol and fat intake. And it's not really surprising, is it? Almost every day brings an update on healthy eating. What was good for us yesterday suddenly becomes bad for us today – and vice versa! My own research demonstrates that people believe they should:

1. Cut overall fat intake.
2. Reduce saturated fat.
3. Avoid foods which contain cholesterol.
and
4. Eat more polyunsaturates.
or
5. Eat no fat at all.

Whilst the first two points are worth noting, three and four are questionable; and the fifth is positively dangerous. Mary was certainly one of those who thought that no fat at all in the diet was a healthy option.

Cholesterol in food has very little if any effect upon the cholesterol in the bloodstream and the marked increase in the use of polyunsaturated oils and spreads may have more to do with margarine manufacturing and marketing hype than with government advice. Cutting all sources of fat from the diet, unless for supervised medical reasons, is nothing short of foolhardy.

The cholesterol myth

For several years, cholesterol has been linked very closely to heart disease risk. But a number of studies have now suggested that the original thinking behind this concern may be flawed. In other words, the experts at the time got it wrong.

The relatively modern complaint of hypercholesterolaemia (elevated cholesterol) has grown up alongside deteriorating diet quality, including high levels of processed and degenerated foods, a reduction in natural fibre content, increased saturated fat intake, and – probably most significant of all – lower levels of a number of important nutrients. But, except in the rarer cases of familial hypercholesterolaemia (where high cholesterol runs in families), high cholesterol on its own is no longer believed to be a risk factor for heart disease. At the time of writing, there are believed to be around 300 or so other likely hazards including high blood fats (triglycerides), blood which is too thick and sticky, the quantity of fibrinogen in blood, the patient's exposure to cigarette smoke, his sodium/potassium balance, bodyweight, activity level, blood pressure, and the quantity of fibre in his diet. All these things are just as important when assessing likely risk. So, of course, are your family history and your inherited ability to deal with cholesterol internally.

Cutting cholesterol-rich foods may cause more problems than it solves if your diet lacks the right amounts of vitamins, minerals or essential fatty acids. A diet can easily become unbalanced, too restricted, too heavily based upon polyunsaturates or too reliant upon packets and tins. As was the case with Mary's diet, most cholesterol- and fat-lowering diets include skimmed milk and low-fat yoghurt; less-than-well-balanced slimmers' meals; low-fat cheeses, low-fat polyunsaturated spreads; and a range of other manufactured and processed low calorie or low cholesterol products. Unfortunately, a great many of these foods contain an horrendous selection of artificial additives and chemical names whilst worthwhile amounts of vitamins, minerals and essential fatty acids may be conspicuous by their absence. Consumers are persuaded to buy such foods because their low fat or cholesterol-free nature is advertised as 'healthy', and because so many of us are influenced by the media obsession with weight loss. In any case, if you cut down too far on cholesterol-containing foods, your body (which needs the stuff to function properly) will manufacture extra cholesterol internally to make up the shortfall!

Most people are aware that there are two major kinds of lipids (fats) in the blood which make up cholesterol. HDLs (which stands for high density lipoproteins) are generally regarded as the good guys. If present in the right amounts, HDLs can control the bad guys (low density lipoproteins or LDLs) and deal with any excesses.

If your total cholesterol is found to be high but you have a correspondingly high HDL to LDL ratio, some experts now believe you are not at risk. So, if you are given a result which your doctor thinks may be a problem, ask whether or not LDL, HDL, triglyceride levels and blood viscosity have also been measured. If LDL is up a bit but the other factors are normal, then risk may be minimal or non-existent. The automatic introduction of a very low-fat diet and/or cholesterol-lowering drugs may be not only unnecessary but, in some cases, positively dangerous.

Inadequate amounts of the good cholesterol could turn out to be a greater risk factor than having too much of the bad stuff (LDL) chugging through your veins. French researchers found that women with low cholesterol (around 4.0 mmol/l) had three times the risk of coronary heart disease than those with a reading of 8.0 mmol/l.

Polyunsaturates may not be so healthy after all

It's true that polyunsaturates can reduce total cholesterol – which is why they have been so vigorously promoted as 'healthy' fats. But too many polys may not be so good for you. In bringing down one kind of cholesterol – the LDL – they unfortunately also lower the beneficial HDL (which helps reduce the risk of heart disease!). In addition, research suggests that large intakes of polyunsaturated fatty acids may depress the immune system.

Liquid polyunsaturated oils are extracted from nuts, seeds, pulses and vegetables by a method called cold-pressing. Quality polyunsaturates produced by this method are rich in essential fatty acids and other nutrients and should be included in the diet.

Cold-pressed (what I always call 'real'), unprocessed polyunsaturates do not, of course, lend themselves well to spreading because they are naturally liquid at room temperature! The polyunsaturates found in margarine-type yellow fats are made by taking the liquid oils and solidifying them by a process called hydrogenation. This turns some of the polyunsaturates into saturates and changes beneficial *cis*-fatty acids found in the unadulterated oil (the biologically active form) into the positively unhealthy *trans*-fatty acids. Trans-fatty acids act like saturates and are

another of the badly behaved blocking factors which inhibit the conversion of essential fatty acids to
prostaglandins. They are also much stickier than the
healthier cis-fatty acids and so have a greater tendency to
glue themselves to artery walls and cause fatty deposits in
various organs. But avoiding them may seem difficult,
especially in a diet which contains lots of processed foods
and hydrogenated fats.

Trans-fatty acids are everywhere: small amounts turn up
in meat and dairy products but by far the largest quantities
come from slimmers' meals, take-aways, packet meals,
cream cakes, doughnuts, gooey pastries, sweets, burgers,
chips, crisps, biscuits, some breakfast cereals, margarines,
and poor quality vegetable oils. Check out a few product
labels and the words 'made from hydrogenated vegetable
oils' will pop up with horrifying regularity. As we have
seen in Chapter 1, it is almost impossible to avoid all the
blocking agents which prevent the uptake of the beneficial
cis-fatty acids, so maybe it's not surprising that essential
fatty acid deficiency is such a common occurrence.

**The quantities and sources of trans-fatty acids in
food:**

Cakes, pastries, biscuits:	up to 38%
Chips:	up to 38%
Margarines:	up to 36%
Cooking oils:	up to 37%

Many other processed foods are made with margarines
and cooking oils and so will also include trans-fatty
acids.

Apart from the damage caused by hydrogenation and
trans-fatty acids, the healthful aspects of polyunsaturated
oils are also at risk from the oxidation which occurs when
they are exposed to heat, light, air or radiation after pur-
chase. For this reason, polys should be stored carefully in a

cool dark place and never used for cooking. Replace the cap securely after use and never leave oils exposed in a hot sunny kitchen.

This information surprises people who believe that food cooked in, say, sunflower oil is likely to be healthier than the same food cooked in butter or other saturated fat. But it really is safer to use cold-pressed polyunsaturated oils only for salads and to avoid hydrogenated fats altogether. Use olive oil for cooking and enjoy small amounts of butter or non-hydrogenated margarine for spreading. Some books recommend sunflower, sesame, safflower and corn oils for frying but it should be borne in mind that these oils (good though they may be for cold uses) contain high levels of polyunsaturated fatty acids which will be damaged in the heating process. Peanut oil should never be used. Peanuts are often contaminated by an aflatoxin fungus which is suspected of being carcinogenic.

Be sensible about saturates

Most of us are familiar with saturated fats, the ones which are naturally solid at room temperature – butter, dripping and lard. Full-fat milk, cream, cheese and fatty meat are all high in saturates. In most people's minds, saturated fat equals cholesterol and research has confirmed repeated links between the two. However, new work suggests that even this advice may need to be modified. Studies show that saturates and cholesterol may be less important than the level of antioxidant nutrients and essential fatty acids in the blood. After all, the 'bad' LDL cholesterol 'misbehaves' only when these protective nutrients are missing. It is the oxidizing of cholesterol and fats which can lead to clogged arteries! So, be sensible about saturates but don't go to extremes or cut them out of your diet altogether.

Monounsaturates

Raw, unrefined extra-virgin olive oil is probably the best known monounsaturate and is certainly a very nutritious and beneficially active oil. Monounsaturates also turn up in avocado pears, almonds, macadamia nuts, pecans and pistachios. Best quality olive oil is stable enough at room temperature to be used for cooking (instead of polyunsaturates).

One of the reasons I recommended olive oil to Mary (who was reluctant to have surgery) is because of its known ability to relieve some cases of gallstones. Such cases were documented during the days of the Roman Empire! The incidence of gallstones is still rare in Southern Italy, where the consumption of olive oil is high.

How much fat is healthy?

It can be difficult to know whether your fat intake is too high or too low. The following is a *very general* guide to a sensible maximum intake:

- No more than a quarter of a pint of semi-skimmed or goat's milk daily.
- Free-range eggs – two or three per week.
- Free-range chicken, turkey or rabbit – two servings per week.
- Fresh oily fish – two servings per week.
- Cold-pressed oils – such as olive oil, walnut or sesame seed oil – 10 fluid ounces per week.
- Additive-free curd cheese – 3 to 4 oz per week.
- Fresh live bio-yoghurt – three small tubs per week.
- Butter – 3 oz per week.
- Lean lamb – one portion per week.
- Lamb's liver – one portion per week.
- Polyunsaturated spreads – keep them to an absolute minimum and use only those which are made with non-hydrogenated vegetable oils (usually available in health food stores).
- Include plenty of fresh fruits, vegetables, seeds, nuts and wholegrains.

To reduce intake of the wrong kind of fats, keep these foods to an absolute minimum:

- Pork and all pork products including ham, sausages, bacon and pork pies.
- Beef and beef products.
- Fatty and deep-fried foods.
- Mayonnaise-laden sandwiches.
- Ice cream.
- Pastries, cakes and biscuits.
- Crisps and peanuts.
- Chocolate.
- Tinned and processed meats.

Getting the balance right

In my own experience with patients, I have found that achieving the right balance of cholesterol, blood fats and viscosity has more to do with introducing sensible supplementation (particularly of GLA and fish oil) and improving intake of fresh fruits, vegetables, cold-pressed oils and wholegrains than indulging in dietary extremes. If you have a problem with high triglycerides or elevated cholesterol or, like Mary, have been suffering with any of the problems associated with low-cal, low-fat dieting, then these tips are well worth following:

- *Don't* give up eggs, unless you have an allergy to egg protein. A couple of free-range eggs per week will give you useful extra nourishment, and nutritious lecithin. There is *no* evidence to support the fear that eggs raise blood cholesterol.
- *Don't* throw the butter-dish away. Small amounts of unsalted or low-salt butter are, in my view, better than lots of artificially manufactured and additive-ridden spreads.
- *Don't* deep-fry *anything*. Stir-fry with extra-virgin olive oil.
- *Don't* eat shop-bought cakes, pastries, pies, biscuits, take-aways, fatty meats or excessive amounts of hard

cheese. If you don't buy them, they won't be in the cup-
board when temptation strikes!

- *Do* be sensible about supplementation. Follow the pack
instructions and don't be tempted to exceed the recommended dosages. More is not necessarily better!
- *Do* learn how to relax. Permanent negative stress and
anxiety thickens your blood. Research carried out in the
United States has shown that type A personalities
(typically highly stressed individuals) have a fifty per
cent greater risk of coronary heart disease. More recent
studies have discovered a link between stress and low
levels of the beneficial HDLs. If you find relaxing difficult, go to a class – get some help. Don't just ignore the
warning signs. There are lots of helpful books and cassette tapes available on how to deal with worry,
depression, panic attacks and excessive stress. You owe
it to yourself to do something about such problems.
- *Do* try to include daily:
  - Evening primrose oil; see Chapter 10 for recommended
  dosages.
  - One gram (1000 mg) vitamin C complex.
  - A tablespoon linseeds.
  - A tablespoon of best quality lecithin granules rich in
  phosphatidyl choline (check the label).
  - Pectin-rich foods such as fresh grapefruit and apples.
  - A tablespoon or two of extra-virgin olive oil.
  - The equivalent of one garlic clove – fresh or as a sup-
  plement.
- *Do* treat yourself to the occasional bar of carob or other
health-food sweet treat such as dried fruit, or nuts and
seeds – and kick the chocolate habit.
- *Do* include plenty of fresh green leafy and root vegetables, salads, fresh oily fish, brown rice, wholewheat
pasta and jacket potatoes regularly in your menu.
- *Do* remember that a diet rich in soluble fibre is particularly helpful in reducing the sticky LDLs, so go for
things like oat bran, brown rice, peas, beans and lentils
too. If you don't like them, hide them in home-made
soups, stews and other baking.

- *Do* try to follow the principles of food combining recommended by Drs William Howard Hay and Herbert Shelton. This is a particularly safe and simple way to shed those excess pounds without counting calories, giving up lots of enjoyable foods or exposing yourself to the health hazards, stresses, guilt and inevitable failure of the latest fad or crash diet. My own food-combining formula which I have used with patients for many years is now in book form, as *The Food Combining Diet* (Thorsons, 1993). See pages 51-54 for more information.

Finally don't lose any sleep if you have just been told your cholesterol is high. Fretting about it won't bring it down but could easily increase your stress levels and your blood pressure! Take heart from one of the many patients who have been here for treatment. This particular lady was almost three stones overweight and had a total cholesterol reading of 12.2 mmol/1. After six months of following the above recommendations, her weight was back to normal and her cholesterol level was a healthy 5.2 mmol/1.

Health Note: If you are really keen to follow a very low fat diet, don't do so for longer than two months unless you are being medically and nutritionally supervised. I always try to persuade patients who want to lose weight to do so safely and sensibly; to follow a healthy eating plan for life rather than the latest diet phenomenon. Be suspicious about anything which promises miracles. And to help repair the damage caused by years of low fatty acid intake, I always recommend a regular supply of GLA.

Evening primrose oil for high blood pressure and heart disease

Regular daily supplements of evening primrose oil (possibly with fish oil capsules) can be very helpful in bringing high blood pressure and cholesterol under control. I believe they are well worth trying before embarking upon potentially hazardous drug medicines. Cholesterol-lowering drugs became the subject of some negative publicity when several international studies uncovered an increased incidence of behavioural problems, mood changes and accidental or violent death amongst the medicated group without there being any significant reduction in risk from heart disease. In other words, the harm caused probably outweighs the good.

The role of essential fatty acids in maintaining heart health is increasingly seen to be important. These vital nutrients – and the prostaglandins which are made from them – are involved in regulating blood pressure and blood cholesterol, preventing the build-up of plaque in the arteries, increasing blood flow and cardiac output, and making sure that the blood is neither too thick nor too thin. Scientists are studying the function of DGLA (dihomo gamma linolenic acid; derived from GLA) and suspect that those at risk from coronary heart and artery disease may have either a deficiency of fatty acids in the diet or a problem converting them to GLA, DGLA and prostaglandins. When evening primrose oil is given, DGLA levels are seen to improve, illustrating that a deficiency of this fatty acid may be an important predictor of heart disease.

Trials are continuing but there is strong evidence to suggest that supplementation with both GLA from evening primrose oil and the parallel EPA and DHA from fish oil may be an important breakthrough both in prevention and treatment. It is estimated that one-third to one-half of the patients who undergo surgery to flush out furred arteries end up with re-narrowed blood vessels within six months of the operation. Test groups who were given fish oil had far less recurrence than those who received no supplement. (Reported in *Circulation* 85(3) (1992), pp.950–5.)

So it seems that the use of direct dietary supplements for heart patients could reduce greatly the risk of cardiac arrest and, if used as a preventive measure, may also cut considerably the possibility of heart disease occurring in the first place.

Your new healthy eating plan

Supplements of evening primrose oil, vitamins and minerals can be a great addition to a healthy diet but are not substitutes for nourishing meals. The quality of the food you eat is vitally important. Use the following lists to help you choose which foods are best and which are not so healthy.

Choose:

- All kinds of fresh salad and vegetables. Don't settle for just lettuce, tomato and cucumber, or cabbage and potato. Most supermarkets and grocery stores now stock a vast range of produce, so be adventurous and put some excitement and interest into your diet. How about artichokes, aubergines, avocado, beetroot, Brussels sprouts, broccoli, calabrese, all kinds of cabbage, carrots, cauliflower, celery, celeriac, cucumber, courgette, chicory, all varieties and colours of lettuce, kale, kohlrabi, leek, onion, parsnips, peas, radishes, squash, swede, turnip, turnip greens and watercress? Try to have a good-sized salad and two or three fresh vegetables every day.
- Sprouted seeds, pulses and grains – try alfalfa, aduki beans, mung beans, fenugreek seeds, lentils, mustard, pumpkin seeds, sesame seeds or chick peas. All are great with salads and easy to grow at home on the kitchen windowsill. For more information on how to produce these tasty, nutrient-rich foods, see Leslie Kenton's *Raw Energy* (Century, 1984).
- Fresh fruits including apples, apricots, bananas, blackberries, blackcurrants, blueberries, bilberries, cherries, grapefruit, rapes, kiwi-fruits, melons, peaches, pears, pineapples, raspberries and satsumas. Aim for two or three pieces of fruit each day, eaten either before or between meals, but not with other food. Fruit is digested more efficiently when eaten on its own.

- Dried fruits are full of fibre and nutrients and they make tasty sweet treats and snacks.
- Fruit tinned in natural juice is a useful standby for emergencies but is still no substitute for fresh. Fruit in syrup should be avoided.
- Make the most of fresh and dried culinary herbs. They are a wonderful source of nourishment. If growing them at home is not possible, remember that most food stores stock a range of fresh herbs. Try chives, chervil, dill, fennel, marjoram, sage, parsley, basil, rosemary, mint, salad burnet, tarragon and thyme.
- Wholegrains (also known as complex carbohydrates are an important part of a healthy eating programme and there are plenty to choose from: barley, brown rice, buckwheat, bulgar wheat, cracked wheat, millet, oat bran, oatmeal, wholewheat pasta, quinoa and rye. When making cakes, pastry, biscuits or bread, choose wholemeal flour instead of white. Aim for one meal each day which is based on wholegrains and serve it with either salad or vegetables.
- Potatoes are full of goodness and jacket potatoes are an excellent source of dietary fibre. However, avoid the skins unless you know they are organic. Enjoy them with vegetables, salads, a spoonful of hummus, a knob of butter or an olive oil and cider vinegar dressing. If life without chips depresses you then try the healthy way. Prepare your chips or sliced potato in the usual manner. Rinse them well in cold water and dry them. Place them in a large bowl and pour over two tablespoons of extra-virgin olive oil and sprinkle with a teaspoon of sea salt. Stir until all the potato is well covered with oil. Then tip them out on to a baking sheet and cook them in a hot oven until golden brown, turning them once or twice during the cooking time. Sweet potato is a tasty, nutritious, satisfying and colourful alternative to boiled, baked or mashed potato but does not lend itself well to chipping.
- Beans and lentils are nourishing foods but are often dismissed because of their tendency to cause indigestion

and other embarrassment! Overcome the problem by preparing and cooking them carefully – and then mixing them only with salads or vegetables, not with meat, fish, eggs, cheese, milk, potato, rice, pasta or bread. Always chew pulse foods thoroughly and slowly.

- Seeds like sesame, sunflower, pumpkin, fenugreek and linseeds are rich in essential fatty acids, vitamins and minerals.
- So too are almonds, brazils, hazlenuts, macadamia nuts, walnuts and pecans.
- These foods provide good quality protein without oodles of fat: low fat bio-yoghurt (make sure it's additive-free), curd cheese (likewise), goat's cheese, buttermilk, free-range poultry, free-range eggs, fresh fish, seafood, rabbit, lean lamb, lamb's liver.
- Cook with extra-virgin olive oil and use small amounts of butter or non-hydrogenated margarine for spreading.
- Although it's wise to keep sugary foods to a minimum, good quality honey, real maple syrup, carob spread, crystallized ginger, dried fruits and blackstrap molasses make useful alternative sweetenings.

Avoid:
Do whatever you can to avoid the foods on the list below.

- Anything fried or fatty.
- Refined and sugar-coated breakfast cereals.
- Wheat bran.
- Beef, pork and all their related products, including burgers and pork pies.
- Tinned and preserved meats.
- Any food which is charcoaled, smoked, seared or burned.
- Ready meals and packeted or tinned food which contain hydrogenated oils or other additives.
- Mayonnaise, ketchup and bottled sauces.
- Look upon crisps, peanuts, chocolate, cola, chips, sticky cakes, pastries, doughnuts, pies and soft drinks as occasional treats only.
- Be moderate about your coffee and tea intake. Two or

three cups per day can be enjoyable and stimulating. More than that and you could be losing valuable nourishment since the tannin, caffeine and other chemicals found in these beverages are well-known vitamin and mineral robbers.

A seven-day diet

If you have been thinking of changing your diet but just haven't come around to it yet, or if you have some extra weight which doesn't want to move, why not have a look at the ideas in this seven-day eating plan? There are no complicated recipes to follow – just simple and basic menu ideas which you can adapt or expand to suit your own lifestyle. They are based upon the principles of food-combining (the Hay system) which has proved to be so beneficial in my husband's recovery from serious illness, and also to many of my patients and former patients. Food-combining is a very safe, sensible and simple way of eating which has been in use for almost a century. By not mixing foods that fight, it helps you lose weight and improves the digestion and absorption of food.

You will see that each day includes three main meals (one starch-based, one protein-based and one which is either just fruit, salad or vegetables). All lunches and dinners are interchangeable. There is no restriction on quantity. Just eat until you are *comfortably* full. In addition to the meals listed, make sure that you eat a piece of fresh fruit as a midmorning snack each day. If you are peckish during the afternoon, snack on some dried fruit, nuts or seeds.

Day one breakfast:
A good-sized tub of plain bio-yoghurt mixed with a teaspoon of dark honey or molasses and a handful of pumpkin seeds.

Day one lunch:
A salad medley made up with as many salad and raw

vegetable items as you like. Try mixing chopped celery, sprouted alfalfa, shredded lettuce, grated raw beetroot and carrot and sliced green peppers. Dress with olive oil and cider vinegar. For more ideas, check the list on page 48.

Day one dinner:
Half a small melon.
(Leave fifteen minutes between starter and main course.)
Large jacket potato served with a tasty topping of stir-fried onions and beansprouts or any stir-fried vegetables.

Day two breakfast:
The other half of the melon.

Day two lunch:
Grilled trout or mackerel garnished with finely sliced fresh ginger and sprinkled with soy sauce.

Day two dinner:
Wholewheat pasta (any shape and quantity) with a large green salad.
(Leave fifteen minutes between courses.)
Follow with fresh banana cream: liquidize a large banana with a tablespoon of fresh single cream.

Day three breakfast:
Two free-range boiled, poached or scrambled eggs (don't have toast, bread or rolls with the eggs).

Day three lunch:
Two wholewheat pitta breads filled with sliced tomato, cucumber and watercress.

Day three dinner:
Vegetable casserole made with carrots, leeks, turnips, swede, onion, red pepper and aubergine.
Leave fifteen minutes between courses and follow with a fresh fruit salad.

Day four breakfast:
Oatmeal porridge: cook the oats in water (not milk) and serve with a teaspoon of maple syrup or honey and two teaspoons of fresh single cream.

Day four lunch:
Fresh fruit medley. Choose any kind of fresh fruit in any quantity or variety. Make sure that all fruit is washed thoroughly and that apples and pears are peeled.

Day four dinner:
Half a ruby grapefruit.
(Leave fifteen minutes between courses.)
Follow with sautéed breast of chicken served with steamed vegetables. Do not include potatoes, rice, pasta, bread or any other starch at this meal.

Day five breakfast:
Wholemeal soda bread served with a little butter and honey or home-made preserve.

Day five lunch:
Omelette with sliced mushrooms served with a green salad.

Day five dinner:
Home-made vegetable soup using any ingredients of your choice.

Day six breakfast:
Dried fruit compote. Buy additive-free mixed dried fruit from the health food store. Prepare the mixture by placing it in a pan with just enough water to cover. Bring quickly to the boil, remove from the heat and allow to soak overnight.

Day six lunch:
Sweet potato and parsnip soup. Wash the vegetables and cut them into small chunks. Cook until tender. Add a quarter of a teaspoon of nutmeg, and a sprinkling of sea

salt and black pepper. When cool enough, liquidize and serve with rye crackers.

Day six dinner:
Stir-fried prawns with mushrooms. Mix thinly-sliced dark skinned mushrooms, ginger, spring onions and yellow peppers and stir-fry them with the prawns in extra-virgin olive oil. Season with a little soy sauce and serve with salad.

Day seven breakfast:
Sautéed mushrooms and tomatoes. Choose large flat mushrooms and slices of skinned tomatoes and cook them in olive oil. Eat as many as you like.

Day seven lunch:
Pineapple salad. Slices of fresh pineapple served with kiwi fruit and curd cheese.
or
Grilled trout with flaked almonds.

Day seven dinner:
Half an avocado pear filled with olive oil and cider vinegar. Brown basmati rice with pine nuts – delicious served hot or cold. Cook the rice and mix it with a handful of pine nuts, sunflower seeds and pumpkin seeds. Serve with mangetout, baby sweetcorn and sliced courgettes.

For more detailed recipe and menu ideas and extra help for easy weight loss, you may find my book, *The Food Combining Diet*, helpful.

Sources:

Smith, Russell L., *The Cholesterol Conspiracy* (Warren H. Green Inc., St Louis, Missouri, 1991).
Ravnskaw U., 'Cholesterol-lowering trials in coronary heart disease: frequency of citation and outcome', *British Medical Journal* 305 (1992), 15–19.

Smith L. L., 'Another cholesterol hypothesis: cholesterol as an antioxidant', *Free Radical Biology & Medicine* 11 (1991), 47–61.

Rath M., Pauling L., 'Solution to the puzzle of human cardiovascular disease: its primary cause is ascorbate deficiency leading to the deposition of lipoprotein(a) and fibrinogen/fibrin in the vascular wall', *Journal of Orthomolecular Medicine 6(3&4) (1991), 125–134.*

'Certain lipid profile predicts CHD in women: elevated triglycerides and HDL as risk factors for heart disease', *Family Practice News 21(23) (1991),* 1.

Sacks F. M., Willet W. W., 'More on chewing the fat: the good fat and the good cholesterol', *New England Journal of Medicine* (12 December 1991), 1740–1.

Mensink R. P., & Katan M. B., 'Effect of dietary trans-fatty acids on high density and low density lipoprotein cholesterol levels in healthy subjects', *New England Journal of Medicine* 323 (1991), 439–435.

Oliver F., 'Might treatment of hypercholesterolaemia increase noncardiac mortality?', *Lancet* (22 June 1991) 1529–31.

Report of the International Conference on Antioxidants – Chemical, Physiological, Nutritional and Toxicological Aspects. American Health Foundation, October 1991.

Antioxidant Vitamins and Beta Carotene in Disease Prevention, International Conference. October 1989.

XIIIth Congress of the European Society of Cardiology, Amsterdam, 18-22 August 1991. Notes.

Ramsay L. E., Yeo W. W., Jackson P. R., 'Dietary reduction of serum cholesterol concentration: time to think again', *British Medical Journal* 303 (1991) 953–7.

Isles C. G., Hole D. J., Gillis C. R. *et al.,* 'Plasma cholesterol, coronary heart disease and cancer in the Renfrew and Paisley survey', *British Medical Journal* 298 (1989), 920–4.

Cameron N. E., Cotter M. A., Robertson S., 'Essential fatty acid diet supplementation. Effects on peripheral nerve and skeletal muscle function and capillarization in streptozocin-induced diabetic rats.', *Diabetes* 40 (1991) 532–9.

Vaddadi K. S., Horrobin D. F., 'Weight loss produced by evening primrose oil administration', *IRCS Medical Science 7 (1979),* 52.

Fanstone T. C. et al., 'Suppression by prostaglandin E1 of vascular permeability induced by vasoactive inflammatory mediators', *T. of Immunology* 125 (1980), 2591–6.

Holborow P. L., 'Melanoma patients consume more polyunsaturated fat than people without melanoma', *New Zealand Medical Journal* (27 November 1992), 502.

Kestin M., Clifton P. M., Rousse I. L., Nestel P. J., 'Effects of dietary cholesterol in normolipidaemic subjects not modified by nature and amount of dietary fat', *American Journal of Clinical Nutrition* 50 (1989), 528–32.

Addis P. B., 'Occurrence of lipid oxidation products in foods', *Fd.Chem.Toxic* 24 (1986), 1021.

Baranowski, Zane, *Free Radicals, Stress, Aging and Antioxidant Enzymes – A Guide to Cellular Health*

Niki E., Yamamoto Y., Komuro E., Sato K., 'Membrane damage, lipid oxidation and antioxidants', *American Journal of Clinical Nutrition* 53 (1991), 201–5.

5

Evening primrose oil for babies and children

A good supply of essential fatty acids is vital to the healthy development of children – from conception onwards! Inside the womb, the growing baby is unable to synthesize fatty acids. Essential fatty acids (from both linoleic and alpha linolenic acid see Chapter 1) must therefore be provided via the mother's circulation through the placenta, making the quality of her pre-conceptual and pregnancy diet vitally important. The post-natal diet should be of equal concern to ensure that, if a mother chooses to breast-feed, her milk contains the fatty acids required for her baby's growth and health.

Fresh oily fish, canned salmon and sardines, lamb's liver, free-range poultry, fresh leafy green vegetables, root vegetables, salads, bio-yoghurt, fresh fruit, brown rice, rye, oats, sunflower seeds, pumpkin seeds, almonds, brazils, olive oil and garlic are all nutrient-dense foods which supply vitamins, minerals, dietary fibre, protein, carbohydrate and the right kind of fats and oils needed for healthy mums. A daily capsule of evening primrose oil (see Chapter 10) may help to ensure beneficial levels of GLA for you and your baby, but you should always check with your medical adviser first.

Don't be persuaded by well-meaning doctors, health visitors or dietitians to drink extra quantities of cow's milk during pregnancy and breast-feeding. This advice is out-moded, outdated, and in my view as a nutrition practitioner, potentially problematic. Although advertised as being a rich source of calcium, this particular mineral is often very poorly absorbed from cow's milk. It always strikes me as rather odd – and unnatural – that we are the only species which, voluntarily, consumes the milk of another species. Cow's milk is very nourishing for calves but to humans it is a common allergen as well as being notoriously mucus-forming. In addition, there is concern that mothers who drink lots of cow's milk during pregnancy may produce children with a greater susceptibility to milk allergy. The foods listed above should provide adequate calcium levels without the need to resort to this dietary troublemaker.

Breast may be best . . .

Human breast milk is an eminently natural source of GLA (gamma linolenic acid) and DHA (docosahexaenoic acid): Mother Nature designed it to provide all the nutrition needed by a new baby for optimum growth and development. In particular, essential fatty acids are vital for the baby's brain and nervous system. A direct source of fatty acids is needed because young babies do not have conversion systems which are mature enough to convert them internally.

Recent research has shown that breast-fed babies are more likely to have an improved level of intellectual development. This may be due to the high level of essential fatty acids found in breast milk compared to that in formula or cow's milk. Studies show that the breast-fed babies of healthy mothers are less likely to experience allergies, gastric disorders, learning difficulties, eczema and other conditions such as colic. In my own experience with patients, such children are also less prone to hyperactivity.

. . . But formulas are improving

This does not mean that all bottle-fed babies are going to suffer with the above conditions (or that breast-fed babies will be immune from them). Not all mums are able to breast-feed, and in such cases it would be reassuring to know that the chosen formula was as close to the composition of breast milk as possible.

Manufacturers are striving constantly to correct the fatty acid inadequacies of commercial formulas, but research into the special nutritional needs of babies demonstrates that formulas have not always provided optimum nourishment.

Dangers to avoid

One way in which some manufacturers' formula feeds attempt to mimic human breast milk is by including the natural milk sugar lactose. However, experts have voiced disquiet that so many baby milk products incorporate varying types and levels of other sugars such as malto-dextrin, glucose syrup and/or amylose either instead of – or in addition to – the lactose.

The campaign group Action and Information on Sugars (AIS) is concerned that highly sweetened milks violate the principle that formulas should resemble breast milk as closely as possible. Whereas lactose is found naturally in breast milk, these other sugars are not. Such unnecessary additions may give a baby a liking for sweet foods and pose a threat to healthy gums and teeth. A sweet tooth acquired early in life can be an almost impossible habit to break!

Tooth decay, according to the Department of Health's COMA report, can be related primarily to non-milk sugars. They advise 'for infants and young children . . . sugars (e.g. sucrose, glucose, fructose) should not be given in feeders where they may be in contact with the teeth for prolonged periods'.

But at the same time that the World Health Organization is recommending that we cut our sugar intake by half, the European Commission is proposing to allow manufacturers of formula to add up to fifty per cent sugar without any compulsion to provide detailed labelling. For example, a feed may contain glucose syrup but, by law,

may be labelled 'sucrose-free'. Such misleading information gives the (deliberate?) impression that the product is
sugar-free when, obviously, it is not.

Labels do not always make it clear that sugar is in the ingredients. Anything ending '-ose' is a sugar – for example,
dextrose, galactose, glucose, sucrose and maltose. Brown
sugar is usually just plain sucrose, even though many
people still think it is better for them than the 'pure white
and deadly' variety. The only brown sugar which contains
any worthwhile nourishment is molasses.

Sugar has the potential to use up and destroy valuable
nutrients. Excess sugars may also be responsible for certain bowel diseases and for an increase in blood sugar
disorders such as diabetes and hypoglycaemia. A study
carried out by the Karolinska Institute in Stockholm,
Sweden, suggests that large amounts of sugar taken when
young could increase the risk of developing ulcerative colitis and Crohn's disease in later life. And hypoglycaemia
(low blood sugar) is a problem not uncommon in newborn
babies and infants.

Sugar is needed by the body for energy but only as the
natural and complex kind found in unprocessed foods.
The adult body works best when fed with a controlled release of sugar from starchy and fibrous foods which are
broken down and assimilated slowly, keeping the blood
glucose levels properly balanced. When eaten to excess,
added sugars and those found in processed and refined
foods cause dramatic and wild fluctuations in blood glucose, increasing the risk of diabetes, hypoglycaemia,
adrenal exhaustion, heart disease and possibly even cancer. The newborn baby's digestive system cannot cope
with dietary fibre and shouldn't be receiving non-milk
sugars, so it relies upon its mother to provide lactose – via
the breast milk or formula. Being vigilant about the (non-
milk) sugar content of formulas and baby feeds is plain
good sense.

Soya milk is sometimes recommended for babies in
cases of cow's milk allergy but, in the view of some pae-
diatricians, it is not a suitable substitute. Soya beans are a

natural, nutrient-packed food but soya drinks are processed. Soya protein molecules are large and difficult for babies to digest, thus causing the nutrients to be poorly absorbed. The Principal Hospital Scientist at the Department of Paediatrics, Flinders Medical Centre in South Australia, Dr Robert Gibson, considers that allergic reactions and immunity problems are more common in soy-fed babies due to the fact that soy proteins are 'alien' to the body. However, Dr Gibson believes that formula feeds could benefit from being supplemented with the fatty acids found in fish oils, evening primrose and borage oils.

Improving on formulas

Assuming you have chosen a formula low in sugar – remember, lactose is the only sweetener your baby needs – you can ensure the essential fatty acid requirements are met by supplementing with GLA (found in abundance in evening primrose oil) and with fish oil capsules. Vegetarians could use linseed oil instead of fish oil, since this is from the same Omega 3 family of essential fatty acids.

I do not, under any circumstances, recommend buying evening primrose oil in liquid form, even though it may appear to be a convenient way to dispense evening primrose oil to babies or anyone else who cannot swallow capsules. Instead, take one or two *capsules* of evening primrose oil, pierce them open with a sterilized needle and, with the cleanest of fingers, massage the contents into the abdomen and inner thighs of the infant. This method can be of particular benefit to hyperactive children who usually find the sensation of massage pleasurable, calming and therapeutic. Whilst not as much oil will be absorbed as would be taken by mouth, some will certainly get through.

The dangers of microwaving

Some studies have questioned the safety of using micro-wave ovens when preparing formula feeds. Despite reassuring noises from manufacturers, there is concern that, during prolonged heating, the amino acid structure of the liquid may be altered with the possibility that such changes could lead to kidney, liver and nervous system damage. In addition, beneficial cis-fatty acids (see Chapter 1) can be turned into the less than desirable trans-fatty acids). And there is, of course, the risk of scalding. During heating by microwaves, the top of the bottle becomes hotter than the base.

In these situations, my personal preference is always to avoid suspected, potential hazards until they are proven unfounded, rather than continue to use them until they are confirmed as risky, unreliable or possibly life-threatening! Hopefully, further studies will be carried out into the amino acid consumption of food before and after micro-waving cooking.

If you are happy to continue microwaving, American researchers from the University of Pennsylvania have suggested safe steps to warming baby milk:

1. Heat a minimum of 4 fluid ounces at one time.
2. Use only formula which has been taken from the fridge.
3. Stand the bottle upright without any seal or cap.
4. Don't heat a 4 fl oz bottle for more than 30 seconds or an 8 fl oz bottle for more than 45 seconds.
5. Remove the bottle and replace the top. Turn and invert the bottle ten times to make sure the heat is evenly distributed.
6. Test for temperature by shaking some milk on to the back of your hand or on to your tongue.

NB: Microwaves are not suitable for sterilizing bottles unless the oven is equipped with a specially designed steam device and the times quoted will vary depending on the power of the oven.

Infant Eczema

Eczema can make a baby's life (and his parents') miserable. Rough, red, sore, itchy and angry skin can mean restless nights, scratchy days and a child who is tetchy and fractious. Although the actual cause of eczema has yet to be determined, it seems that a straightforward deficiency of essential fatty acids; food intolerance; digestive or absorptive malfunction; or an inherited inability to convert essential fatty acids into prostaglandins hold the most likely answers. Evening primrose oil has been tested very successfully with adults, babies and young children and has given relief to eczema's distressing symptoms in the majority of cases. Evening primrose oil has been available on prescription for the treatment of eczema since 1988, so if any member of your family has the condition it could be worthwhile seeing your GP. (See 'Improving on formulas', above, for advice on administering the oil to infants.)

Hyperactivity

Extensive surveys carried out by the Hyperactive Children's Support Group have found repeated links between essential fatty acid deficiency and hyperactivity or ADHD (attention-deficit hyperactivity disorder). Dramatic improvements have been documented when previously uncontrollable youngsters were given supplements of GLA together with certain dietary changes. One success story from my own practice is that of Nigel.

The first time Nigel visited my clinic with his mother and father, he proceeded to take the room apart. Anything which was less than ten tons in weight and not fixed to the floor was moved or dismantled by this uncontrollable nine-year-old. Nigel slept for only two or three hours in every twenty-four, his exhausted mother told me. She and her husband were at the end of their tether.

After carrying out some tests and arranging for Nigel to see a doctor colleague who specialized in the treatment of food intolerance, we recommended that all food colourings and sugar were removed from Nigel's diet. He was prescribed evening primrose oil and zinc for three months.

At the second visit, Nigel was almost unrecognizable. He was quiet, polite and attentive and brought me a painting which he had done at school. 'The first one he has ever sat still long enough to complete', said his delighted mum. Nigel's teacher is convinced that, without the nutritional treatment, he would have had to be moved to a special class at the beginning of the next term because he had been so disruptive and aggressive toward other children. The zinc therapy has now finished but Nigel continues to follow an additive-free diet and takes a children's multivitamin capsule and his evening primrose oil every day

Getting the balance right

It is vital to get expert help when treating a hyperactive child. Food additives seem to be a continual hazard, not helped by an EC directive (agreed by the UK Government) which proposes to attach a further fifty additives to the list of those already permitted in baby foods. However, the good news is that some suppliers are taking positive steps to make organic baby foods available.

The removal from the diet of suspect food allergens (corn, wheat, sugar and colourings are just a few of the most common ones) needs to be carefully monitored and is best done with the support of a practitioner who is familiar with nutritional treatments. Taking too many foods away from the child's diet may result in an imbalance of nutrients and consequent inadequate nourishment.

Deficiencies of (or a greater need for) zinc and other nutrients are not uncommon in hyperactive children, but supplementing vitamins and minerals in isolation and without the support of a healthy allergen-free diet may cause more problems than it solves. It cannot be emphasized too strongly that any dietary manipulation or the introduction of supplements must be managed with care. Expert and professional assistance is essential. Unqualified allergy therapists – however well meaning – may be hazardous to your child's health.

Ensuring adequate levels of essential fatty acids in the pre-conceptual diet, during pregnancy and breast-feeding and in the baby's diet too, may be one of the ways to help reduce the risk of hyperactivity. I have certainly noticed significant improvements in hyperactive youngsters whose daily diets have been supplemented with evening primrose oil and multivitamins. You'll find useful addresses and other information at the end of this chapter. The Hyperactive Children's Support Group is particularly helpful – and highly regarded.

Alcoholism – a link between hyperactivity and essential fatty acid deficiency?

The Hyperactive Children's Support Group has come up with startling evidence that untreated hyperactivity may lead to alcoholism in later life! Alcohol appears to produce a fleeting rise in Series 1 prostaglandins which is then followed by a sharp fall in these particular prostaglandins. The symptoms of this dramatic drop in levels is the hangover – one reason why taking evening primrose oil before drinking can help to prevent hangovers happening. Early evidence shows that the addiction to and craving for alcohol may be controlled by the use of GLA.

A vital diet for life

According to American doctor and nutritionist Jeffrey Fisher, heart disease begins in childhood – often in those as young as five years old – and death from heart failure is happening to ten- and twelve-year-olds. Not surprisingly, a link has been established between the furring-up of arteries in youngsters and popular high-fat snacks, take-aways and sugar-laden junk.

In a New York study of more than 200 five- and six-year-old children, results showed high blood pressure, high blood fats and alarming levels of obesity and general lack of fitness. The seriousness of the situation has increased the clamour for more nutrition education for both children and parents. The Expert Panel on Blood Cholesterol Levels in Children and Adolescents in the US suggests an increase in fresh fruits, green and root vegetables, wholegrains, moderate amounts of lean poultry (without the skin) and fresh fish, with an overall reduction in fat intake. Excess saturated fats and trans-fatty acids, of course, can block the natural formation of GLA and thus Series 1 prostaglandins in the body (see Chapter 1) – which is where evening primrose oil supplements can help.

The fast-paced lifestyle of the late twentieth century, with its fast food, convenient ready-meals, and heavily promoted high-fat and high-sugar snacks have all contributed to the demise of regular nourishing meals for children. Busy parents cannot even rely on the once-certain school dinner – not always perfect but nonetheless consistent.

The subject of school dinners can be an emotive one. It seems that one either loves them or hates them. I hated them. It probably had something to do with my aversion to lumpy mashed potato, gristly mince, and tapioca pudding that one could stand the spoon up in. There are schools who manage to produce excellent and nourishing meals every day for their charges and I know many children who thoroughly enjoy their school comestibles. But institutionalized food has gained an unfortunate reputation (sometimes amply justified) of resembling unappetizing slop. Much of it is produced at a central location and shipped out to schools (and hospitals) many miles away. The quality of the chosen ingredients may be questionable: many are tinned and processed. Since meals are kept hot for prolonged periods or reheated on arrival, there will be an inevitable and significant loss of nutrients.

Visually, the meal has often assumed a less than impressive appearance. Hot food turns up tepid, salads lukewarm and limp. But even in these circumstances, school dinners can still be warming, satisfying and comforting.

Constant cuts in funding and the accelerating demise of the school meals service can mean many youngsters going without food at lunchtime. Some schools do provide snacks in place of cooked meals, but the variety is often limited to crisps, biscuits, chocolate, canned drinks and other junk. And where there is a choice of cooked meals, children are more likely to choose burgers and chips whilst avoiding vegetables and salads. Often, this type of food is eaten 'on the hoof' and too quickly. It offers plenty of sugar, salt and fat and so seems filling and satisfying, but contains little in the way of goodness. The low nutrient quality and high levels of additives can encourage hyperactivity, behavioural disorders, lack of concentration and an increased risk of viral infection. Some experts believe that the ready availability of junk food may even be partly responsible for escalating vandalism and violence in the schools and on the streets.

Twelve-year old James had a history of hyperactivity and bad behaviour at school. He was labelled 'uncontrollable' and was sometimes banished to a room on his own, away from other children. With the help of a nutritionist, James' mother discovered that the hyperactivity was caused by sugar and food colourings.

'James takes a packed lunch to school now. Before this, he was having cooked lunch in the canteen and was buying sweets and chocolate from his tuck shop. But it was impossible for him to avoid such things as the sugar and colourings in tinned peas, blancmange and other foods which the school provided. I have encouraged him to learn more about the quality of the food he chooses and he enjoys helping me to prepare his lunch box. Now that he is older, he understands why he has a special diet and is pretty good about keeping to it. The other day in the supermarket he pointed to a bottle of orange squash in someone else's trolley and knew that it contained E102, the dreaded Tartrazine. I was very proud of that. The nutritionist found that he also had a zinc deficiency. He now takes a low-dose, additive-free multivitamin (which contains zinc) every day and also seems to benefit from having 500 mg of vitamin C complex. And he never misses his daily dose of three capsules of evening primrose oil.'

Dehydration danger

Whilst much attention is paid to children's food intake, little if any comment is made about the fluids they consume. Many of today's most attractive drinks for older children are coloured, carbonated and sweetened, either artificially or with unbelievably high levels of sugar – and are often accompanied by salty snacks such as crisps or peanuts. After such a snack a child may rush around the playground or the sports field and then forget to drink. Fluids are quickly lost from the body, especially in hot weather, leading to dehydration, poor elimination and potential kidney problems.

The Sandwich-box solution

Preparing packed lunches is an extra job for an already busy – probably exhausted – parent. But they are a first-class way of making sure that you are providing the best kind of nourishment for your growing child; older kids might be encouraged to choose and to prepare their own healthy midday meal.

- Make sure your tearaway has access to good quality fluids at school or suggest he or she takes a drink with them every day. How about organic apple juice, grape juice or cranberry juice, filtered water, vegetable juices or vegetable soups? (a good way to feed valuable vegetables to children who just won't eat their greens!).
- Fresh fruit. Make sure it is washed thoroughly and, if

possible, discard any skin. Bananas are particularly good – nourishing and easy to peel.

Cautionary tales

Remember that very high-fibre cereals and low-fat foods are not suitable for children under the age of five. Also, don't give whole nuts to youngsters – they could easily choke on them. Some children enjoy ground, crushed nuts mixed with a little honey and used as a spread.

Don't be tempted to bribe a petulant child with sweets or chocolate. Sugar encourages cavities, destroys nutrients in the body, risks hyperactivity and upsets the balance of glucose in the blood – increasing the likelihood of hypoglycaemia and diabetes.

Check Chapter 10 for the recommended dosages of evening primrose oil for children. And, if possible, make sure that the child also takes a multivitamin/mineral supplement suitable for his or her age group.

- Home-made live yoghurt is very cheap to make and can be sweetened with a little organic honey or mashed banana. Travels well in a spill-proof picnic beaker.
- Organic wholemeal bread can be used for sandwiches. Avoid it, however, if your child shows any allergic reactions to wheat, yeast or gluten.
- Canned pink salmon, sardines or sild
- Edam cheese or curd cheese
- Slices of cooked (free-range) chicken
- Tahini spread
- Hard-boiled egg (free-range only)
- Any kind of salad filling
- Hummus
- Rice cakes or oat cakes are useful alternatives if a youngster has a wheat allergy, and are as tasty with savoury or sweet spreads. Experiment with organic peanut butter, curd cheeses, sugar-free preserves, mashed banana or honey.
- Home-made scones, buns, cakes and biscuits are

usually much healthier than the shop-bought variety
and make a good filling sweet treat for a lunch box.
- Dried fruit bars, sesame halva, real liquorice sticks,
crunchy bars, dried fruit, carob bars and fresh fruit
make useful sweet treats.

Useful addresses:

FORESIGHT – The Association for the Promotion of Pre-Conceptual
Care, The Old Vicarage, Church Lane, Witley, Godalming,
Surrey, GU8 5PN. Please send a large envelope and 50p in
stamps.
Hyperactive Children's Support Group, (HACSG), 71 Whyke Lane,
Chichester, West Sussex, PO19 2LD. Valuable source of informa-
tion on how to cope with a hyperactive allergic child. Please send
a large envelope and 50p in stamps.

Useful reading:

Wholefood Childrens' Packed Lunches (The Wholefood Cookery School;
75p including postage and packing from The Vegetarian Society,
Parkdale, Dunham Road, Altrincham, Cheshire WA14 4QG).
Lobstein, Tim, *Children's Food* (Thorsons).
Pay, Joanna, *Cooking For Kids The Healthy Way* (Thorsons).
Mindell, Earl, *The Vitamin Bible For Your Children*.
Hunt, Janet, *The Vegetarian Lunchbox* (Thorsons, 1986).
Lobstein, Tim, *Fast Food Facts* (Camden Press, 1988).

Sources:

Gibson R. A., Kneebone G. M., 'Fatty acid composition of human
colostrum and mature breast milk', *Am.J.Clin.Nutr.*
34 (1981), 252–7.
Friedman Z., 'Essential fatty acid requirements for term and preterm
infants' in *Lipids in Modern Nutrition* (Raven Press, New York,
1987), 79–92.
Gibson R.A., 'Special fats in formula; are they necessary?' *Infant
Nutrition Update Symposium* (notes) (2 July 1990).
Lubec G., Wolf C., Bartosch B., 'Amino acid isomerization and
microwave exposure' (paper on the potential hazards of micro-
wave cooking, in particular of infant formulas), *Lancet* 2 (1989),
1392–3.
'Sugar in baby milks', *Food Magazine* 2(13) (1991), 2.
'Infant formulas', *Food Magazine* 2(17) (1992) 6.
'Herbal baby drinks', *Food Magazine* 2(15) (1991), 12–14.

Comblath M., Schwartz R., Aynsley-Green A., *et al.*, 'Hypoglycaemia in infancy; the need for a rational definition', *Paediatrics* 85(50) (1990), 834–6.

Weiss G., 'Hyperactivity in childhood', *New England Journal of Medicine* 323(20) (1990), 1413–15.

Melnik B. C., & Plewig G., 'Is the origin of atopy linked to deficient conversion of Omega 6 fatty acids to prostaglandin E1?' *J.Am. Acad.Derm.* 21(1-2) (1989), 557–63.

6

More than skin deep

Paula worked as a telephonist on a busy company switch-board. When a promotion to the reception desk was offered to her, she refused because she didn't want to be seen in public. The reason? Her severe eczema.

Paula first came to see me in 1989 after a colleague at work had suggested that a change of diet had helped her own skin condition. Paula was sceptical about treatment but decided to come along 'just for a chat'. The eczema was particularly prevalent on her elbows, knees, calves and the sides of her face and neck. It seems that she had tried a variety of creams and medicines, but although there had been some relief from the itching and irritation, nothing had helped long-term.

The recommendations I made to Paula included cutting out cow's milk and wheat bran from her diet (two very common allergens which seem to aggravate skin prob-lems), eating more seeds, fresh vegetables and fruit, and replacing some red meat meals with oily fish. I also sug-gested six capsules of evening primrose oil and three of fish oil daily. Ten months after beginning the treatment, Paula had one small patch of eczema on the back of her neck and another at the base of her spine. The remainder cleared up completely!

Before treatment, Paula was reluctant to socialize. She believed that she was an embarrassment to her friends and so stayed at home every evening and most weekends. Now, her mother tells me, Paula has 'really come out of her shell. She is far happier and never depressed like she used to be.'

Paula had suffered from eczema for most of her life but

until she talked to me no one had explained the reasons for her condition. Having her questions answered, she told me, helped her to understand and to cope more easily. She was particularly interested in evening primrose oil and wanted to know why, when it had already been available for quite some time, she was still being offered steriod drugs as a first-line treatment.

I explained to Paula that there are two kinds of eczema. Contact eczema (commonly known as contact dermatitis) is caused by external irritants such as chemicals or cosmetics. Contact eczema is obviously more likely to improve if the contact irritant is avoided, but evening primrose oil can also help by strengthening the skin structure so it resists damage.

Atopic eczema is regarded by many experts as an external sign of an internal disorder related to both a malfunctioning immune system and a defective enzyme function. Symptoms include inflammation, itching, flaking and dryness, with a tendency in more severe cases to weeping blisters and scaliness on any part of the body but especially (as in Paula's case) on the face, arms, legs, elbows, knees and ears. Food intolerance, nutrient deficiency, bottle-feeding and cow's milk allergy may be involved in either causing or aggravating the tendency to atopic eczema.

Eczema is believed to affect increasing numbers of the population and estimates suggest more than ten per cent of Britons will develop a skin condition such as eczema at some point during their lives. With so many side effects associated with the palliative orthodox treatments available, the discovery that something as natural and safe as evening primrose oil can relieve eczema should be very welcome. The reason for its effectiveness is not totally understood but is believed to be because eczema patients can't convert the essential fatty acids in food into usable GLA, thus helpful Series 1 prostaglandins, because they lack the essential enzyme delta-6-desaturase. Evening primrose oil bypasses this problem by putting GLA into the body in its usable form. In some eczema sufferers there may be also a straightforward dietary deficiency of essential fatty acids, making supplements even more obviously the answer.

I have studied in great detail and with much interest the mountains of scientific literature which support the use of evening primrose oil as an eczema treatment. What these trials show – and what I have also found in practice – is that larger doses of the oil work better than smaller ones for this condition, especially in the early stages of treatment. This is why, when you check the chapter on dosage, you will see that a higher intake is recommended for eczema; and it is the reason for the large quantity which I prescribed for Paula. So convincing have been the clinical trial results that evening primrose oil has been available on prescription for eczema since 1988.

Action-plan for eczema

In addition to their daily evening primrose oil supplements, eczema sufferers may benefit further if they follow these guidelines:

- Take probiotics (such as *Lactobacillus acidophilus*) to improve bowel function and strengthen immunity.
- Improve diet quality (see Chapter 4) and avoid common allergens such as cow's milk, oranges, orange juice, wheat, yeast, sugar, strawberries and corn.
- Ask for professional nutritional help with food intolerances, digestive disorders and constipation.
- Take time to rest, relax and exercise.
- Increase your intake of oily fish or take supplements of fish oil.
- Avoid irritant clothing fibres, particularly thermal-treated fabric, wool and mohair.
- Avoid ordinary soap and chemicals. Choose washing suds and fabric softeners which are designed especially for sensitive skin.

- Avoid very hot water and sudden changes in temperature.
- Enjoy the fresh air and daylight as often as possible.
- If your skin is suffering from dryness and poor condition and you yourself are feeling tired and run down, try the cleansing diet later in this chapter.

Caring for your skin

Skin diseases like Paula's are discouragingly common. So too are the less serious but nonetheless dispiriting problems such as blemished, oily or dry skin. Unfortunately, most of us tend to take our skin for granted and don't even know how or why it functions as it does.

Eighty per cent of women believe they have a skin problem and the majority say that their skin is sensitive. And they spend millions of pounds every year on a great variety of products, many of which promise to reduce wrinkling and improve condition. But cosmetics and skin treatments can (temporarily) only enhance the surface. To promote really healthy skin, we need to nurture the deeper layers.

The essential fatty acids in evening primrose oil are natural nutrients of the skin, making this super-special oil a near-perfect internal cosmetic. Regular use can improve skin smoothness and texture, protect against the drying effects of wind, sun, air-conditioning and pollution, and may help in increasing moisture retention. Even oily skins can benefit – and, as we saw earlier, the results of evening primrose oil supplementation in the relief of eczema and other skin disorders has been nothing short of astonishing.

Skin structure

Every square inch of skin contains millions of cells. The two and a half square yards which it takes to cover the whole body is a complex structure designed to detect sensation – such as temperature and touch – to protect internal organs from outside damage and harmful bacteria, and to assist in ridding the system of wastes and toxins. When healthy skin is injured, it has an incredible capacity for self-healing. Indeed, there is a tendency to take for granted the amazing fact that burns, cuts, grazes and bruises disappear within a very short space of time, leaving no trace. It is only when afflicted by persistent flaking, itching, irritation, inflammation, deep wounds, excess oil, spots, boils or blemishes that we give thought to our skin's welfare.

The best description I have heard of how skin looks in cross section is Liz Earle's in her excellent book *Save Your Skin with Vital Oils* (Vermilion, 1992). She likens it to a jam sandwich, which has an upper and lower layer stuck together with a fine intermediary filling in between. That upper layer is the one we usually pay most attention to with our cleansers, toners, moisturisers, scrubs, masks and make-up.

Called the epidermis, this outside skin is made from a layer of keratin cells which, although dead, provide tough waterproofing properties and reduce moisture loss from the tissues beneath. The 'jam' is a layer of basal cells which move upwards to replace the shedding epidermal cells. They also convert protein building-blocks (amino acids) into the skin's natural colouring called melanin. This pigment is the body's defence against damage from ultra-violet radiation. The deeper 'underneath' skin is the other side of the sandwich called the dermis, the living level interspersed with blood vessels, sweat glands, hair follicles and sebaceous glands and supported by a network of collagen and elastin fibres which make up the connective tissue. The sebaceous and sweat glands provide the skin with lubricants and the blood vessels and capillaries transport the nutrients which the skin needs to live and breathe.

Skin cells are in a constant state of flux, working their way from the dermis to the epidermis. As old cells flake away, they are replaced by new cells from the layers below; the condition of the skin which you can see depends largely upon the fitness of the hidden but very active *dermis*. As skin ages, however, each cell's ability to reproduce and renew itself decreases. In some skin disorders, cells rush to the surface too quickly and proliferate (as in psoriasis); in others, they don't move fast enough, resulting in blocked pores and inadequate elimination of wastes.

Nourishing the skin

The key to healthy skin is to encourage healthy and balanced cellular renewal. To keep it strong and supple and to enable it to resist disease, skin must be able to rely on a reliable store of nourishment. Skins which age less quickly tend to have a more efficient cell turnover which, in turn, will be directly affected by the quality of nutrients they receive. In addition, the rate of ageing will be influenced by the external environment including sun and wind exposure, atmospheric moisture levels and central heating. If the skin is adequately nourished from the inside, it will develop far greater resistance to these ravages.

The importance of essential fatty acids

Every single cell in the body needs essential fatty acids to feed and support its structure; almost every single biological process requires prostaglandins to make it happen. So what chance does someone have of continued and long-term good health if they are lacking in essential fatty acids? When the body doesn't consume enough essential fatty acids, or has difficulty converting them into active substances, the resulting deficiencies will lead, almost inevitably, to some kind of malady. An interesting observation from early animal studies shows that, with increasing age, there is a reduced supply of fatty acids to the skin, resulting in a reduction in its health, plumpness and smoothness.

The skin reacts very quickly to nutrient deficiency and is well known for being a very visible health indicator. When a lack of essential fatty acids affects internal organs, there may be no obvious or immediate indication that trouble is brewing, but the texture, colour and condition of the skin can offer a valuable insight into inner health.

The overall tendency of any skin to be dry or oily is determined by a person's genes. But by taking the right action, it is perfectly possible to encourage disobedient skin to behave in a more balanced and normal way.

Dealing with dry skin

The essential fatty acids (such as those found in evening primrose oil) are among the major keys to preventing moisture loss and so are vital factors in the fight against dry skin conditions. The lipid membrane surrounding each cell and the lipid film which coats and protects the epidermis are both fed by essential fatty acids. This barrier breaks down with age and where there is nutrient deficiency; skin is then not so well protected and can become thinner, more fragile and sensitive. Studies demonstrate that supplements of evening primrose oil lessen the risk of such damage, reduce dryness and increase skin smoothness.

There are a number of other nutrients which help essential fatty acids to work more efficiently and provide important support for dry skin conditions. For example, bioflavonoids are valuable for strengthening capillaries and, with vitamin C, help to maintain the firmness and resilience of collagen and elastin fibres. These two nutrients are often found to be lacking in people who bruise easily, have broken thread veins or prematurely sagging skin. Vitamins A and E act as protective antioxidants against the ravages of ageing and are a real boon to flaking or scaling skin and where cuts and grazes are slow to heal. Vitamin E also helps skin to retain moisture and is a well known remedy for both new and old scars. The trace mineral selenium helps protect lipid membranes from damaging oxidation.

A cleansing diet to revitalize your skin

Regular use of this short-term cleansing diet (for one or two days at a time) will give your skin a real treat, rest your digestion, and cleanse your tissues. It also helps to boost flagging energy. For a whole week before you begin, try to cut down on – or avoid altogether – coffee, cola, chocolate, tea, alcohol, salt and cigarette smoke. And drink plenty of filtered or bottled water.

Stick to the following recommendations for either twenty four or forty eight hours, counting from lunchtime on the first day. In other words, have your normal breakfast on day one and start the cleansing programme at midday.

Day one breakfast:
Eat what you usually have. Your cleansing routine doesn't begin until lunchtime.

Day one lunch:
Choose any crisp and fresh salad items and eat as much as you like. How about chicory, celery, cucumber, grated raw beetroot and carrot, parsley, watercress, spring onion, green peppers, tomato and radish with any fresh culinary herbs which may be available? Dress with extra-virgin olive oil and cider vinegar.

Day one mid-afternoon snack:
A peeled apple and a large glass of organic apple juice.

Day one evening meal:
Begin with a kiwi fruit followed by a large bowl of home-made vegetable soup. It's quick and simple to prepare: chop a leek, an onion, two carrots, a small turnip, a parsnip and a potato. Put them in a pan and cover with filtered

water. Simmer until tender and then mash or liquidize the mixture. Serve with a sprinkle of soy sauce and a few chopped herbs.

If you are hungry during the evening, eat a banana chopped up with some dried figs.

Day two:
Start the day with a large tumbler of water.

Day two breakfast:
Two pieces of fruit, for example, peeled pears, apples, or kiwi fruits, or a large bunch of well-washed grapes.

Day two mid morning snack:
A banana.

(If you decide not to continue any further, go back to normal eating at this point.)

Day two lunch:
Half an avocado pear filled with hummus.

Day two evening meal:
Vegetable sauté. 4 oz broccoli/calabrese and 4 oz cauliflower broken into small florets, one thinly sliced leek, 1 carrot and one stick of celery. Heat a tablespoon of olive oil in a wok or large pan and add the vegetables, stirring constantly until they are *al dente*. Serve on a bed of brown basmati rice.

Day three breakfast:
Dried fruit compote followed by a small tub of live bio-yoghurt.

- If you feel hungry at any time during these three days, snack on any salad or fresh fruit or grab a handful of sunflower and pumpkin seeds. Fruit is a concentrated energy source which helps to flush out accumulated toxins. Fresh salads and vegetables are cleansing and seeds are packed with nutrients including fatty acids.
- Drink as much water as you can between meals – preferably filtered.

- For more information on skin care for particular skin types and on super nutrition for skin, hair and nails, read my new book, *Super Skin* (Thorsons, 1993).

Super healthy hair and resilient nails

Whatever condition makes you decide to take evening primrose oil, one of the first things you are likely to notice is an improvement in hair condition and nail strength. Your fingernails, toenails and your hair are very similar in structure – being made, like your skin, from a protein substance called keratin. For them to remain healthy, good circulation and a constant supply of nutrients are vital – and one of the most important groups for these parts of your body is essential fatty acids which provide toughness, flexibility and protection from damage.

Evening primrose oil may be particularly helpful if you suffer from any of the following conditions:

- Dry hair
- Split ends
- Damaged hair caused by bleaching, perming or colouring
- Dandruff
- Scaly scalp
- Itchy scalp
- Oily hair
- Brittle, flaking, peeling or ridged nails
- Split or bleeding cuticles

Apart from taking evening primrose oil internally, you can use it on the outside too! It can be especially helpful as a nail and hair conditioner.

Once a week, pierce open two or three capsules and massage the contents into the scalp. Wrap your head in a warm towel and leave on for an hour or two. Then wash and condition in the usual way. Surprisingly, this won't make oily hair any oilier. Quite the contrary. The action of the massage and the nutritious oil seem to reduce sebum production and help control oiliness.

Massaging the contents of one capsule into the nails and fingers before going to bed will help to speed the repair process. Toenails will also benefit from this treatment and are less likely to grow inwards if massaged regularly with evening primrose oil.

Sources:

Plummer N., *Lactic Acid Bacteria – Their Role in Human Health* (Biomed Publications Ltd., Westminster House 189–90 Stratford Road, Shirley, Solihull, West Midlands, England B90 3AQ; ISBN 0–9520440–0–5 1992.

Burton J. L., 'Dietary fatty acids and inflammatory skin disease', *Lancet* (7 January 1989), 27–30.

Manku M. S., Horrobin D. F., Morse N. L., Wright S. & Burton J. L., 'Essential fatty acids in the plasma phospholipids of patients with atopic eczema', *British Journal of Dermatology* 110 (1984), 643–8.

Rivers J. P. W., Frankel T. L., 'Essential fatty acid deficiency', *British Medical Bulletin* (1981). Copy kindly provided for me by Scotia Pharmaceuticals.

Ziboh V. A. and Chapkin R. S., 'Metabolism and function of skin lipids', *Progress in Lipid Research* 27 (1988), 81–105.

Stewart J. C., 'Treatment of severe and moderately severe atopic dermatitis with evening primrose oil', *Journal of Nutritional Medicine* 2 (1991), 9–15.

Bordoni A., Biagi P. L., Masi M., Ricci G., Fanelli C., Patrizi A., Ceccolini E., 'Evening primrose oil (Efamol) in the treatment of children with atopic eczema', *Drugs Exptl.Clin.Res.* XIV(4) (1987), 291–7.

Morse P. F., Horrobin D. E. *et al.*, 'Objective assessment of the effects of Epogam on skin smoothness as assessed by profilometry in both normal controls and patients with atopic eczema', *Fat Science TEchnology* 7 (1988), 268–71.

Harvey R. G., 'Management of feline miliary dermatitis by supplementing the diet with essential fatty acids', *Veterinary Record* (6 April 1991), 326–30.

Sampson H., 'Role of immediate food hypersensitivity in the pathogenesis of atopic dermatitis', *J. Allergy Clin.Immunology* 71 (1983), 473–80.

Schalin-Karrila M., Matila L., Jansen C. T. & Uotila P., 'Evening primrose oil in the treatment of atopic eczema: effect on clinical status, plasma phospholipid fatty acids and circulating blood prostaglandins', *British Journal of Dermatology* 117 (1987), 11–19.

Melnik B. C. & Plewig G., 'Is the origin of atopy linked to deficient conversion of Omega 6 fatty acids to prostaglandin E1?' *J.Am. Acad.Derm.* 21(1-2) (1989) 557–63.

7

Relax into health

There is no doubt that being an overanxious coiled spring, loaded with tension and ready to fly off the handle at whoever is nearest or dearest is not good for your long-term health. Excessive amounts of negative stress can make you ill. And illness creates more stress. Fail to deal with this vicious circle and you could be shortenng your life.

More than 100 years ago, physicians were suggesting that significant life events might increase the risk of serious disease. The trauma of bereavement, divorce, redundancy, moving house or being burgled, for example, are some of the more serious and dreaded shocks which many of us have to face but wish that we didn't. How our bodies cope with these kinds of blows could well determine what happens to our health and wellbeing in the long term. Studies continue to show that stressed individuals are more likely to go down with something than those who are calmer. The pressure to perform and compete, the fear of losing one's job, and worries about an uncertain financial future are the major factors blamed for increased stress at work. Almost any change in routine or environment can lead to edginess, palpitations, poor concentration, excess sweating, insomnia, depression and the desire to be somewhere – or even someone – else.

One of the most significant hazards of long-term stress or sudden shock is the negative effect they have on the immune system. Depress this active army of dedicated defenders and the body can find itself more susceptible to colds, flu and other infections as well as more chronic conditions such as irritable bowel syndrome, colitis, eczema, arthritis and heart disease. I find it fascinating that so many of these same conditions can also be linked to a lack of essential fatty acids.

Alan is forty-eight and runs his own business. He was referred to me by his GP for help with 'excessive stress and acute depression'. Alan described himself as 'normally cool, calm and collected' but recently had become over-tired and anxious 'about everything'. His excessive workload had meant missed meals, lots of not-so-healthy snacks and take-aways. He knew he was eating badly and sleeping badly. Noise disturbed him greatly and he had begun to snap at everyone around him. He couldn't con-centrate and felt unusually jumpy.

I gave Alan lots of health tips to help him identify parti-cularly stressful areas and learn how best to cope with them (see the Action-plan for stress at the end of this chapter). I suggested that, in the short term, he take a non-addictive herbal sleeping tablet about an hour before bed and also a regular multivitamin/mineral complex and three capsules of evening primrose oil with his breakfast. He also promised to try and improve his eating habits, to take regular meals and to cut down on the junk food.

Alan's greatest concern was that the undue stress might affect his heart. He'd heard all the usual horror stories about stressed executives dying prematurely from a heart attack and was not convinced by the results of a thorough examination at his doctor's surgery which pronounced his heart perfectly healthy.

Caveman stress

The heart suffers under stress because of the hormones (yes, those again) which are produced in response to anxiety or fear; a prehistoric relic which gave early man the much-needed energy increase to either face the danger or run from it as quickly as possible; the well known 'fight or flight' syndrome. Adrenalin, noradrenalin and cortisol are injected automatically into the bloodstream from the adre-nal glands at the first sign of danger. Heart and pulse rates

quicken, blood pressure and blood sugar go up (all to supply staying power and speed) and the blood itself thickens
– another evolutionary trick to reduce the risk of bleeding
to death should our Palaeolithic predecessor be injured.
The physical activity which is involved in fighting or flee-
ing burns off any excess and unwanted hormones which
may still be in the bloodstream and the system returns
quickly to normal.

Modern man stress

But what if, like Alan, twentieth century stress is getting
you down? What happens if you experience a stress attack
whilst driving the car or at work? There is rarely an oppor-
tunity – or any thought given – to working off the anger,
alarm or exasperation. Emotions are bottled up and the
body stays shocked, distressed and ready for action. Instead of returning to a normal relaxed state, everything
remains on red alert. And in these circumstances, energy
reserves are quickly depleted; no wonder stress goes hand
in hand with fatigue.

Women, far more than men, have the inbuilt mother wit
to cry in response to these kinds of circumstances. Crying
(and laughing) releases physical as well as emotional tension. Far from being a sign of weakness, expressing
emotion is the body's intelligent response to distress.
Shedding tears helps to discharge the toxic burden which
stress puts on the system. Telling people to pull themselves together could, apart from causing other long-term
emotional damage, increase the risk of illness. For
example, the 'stiff upper lip' reluctance to show feelings
and share problems may provide an explanation for early
heart attack in stressed business executives.

Not all stress is bad for you

Positive stress is a different feeling altogether. Pleasurable
excitement, stimulation, the elation of achievement or

anticipation, looking forward to something instead of dreading it, all these things are constructive and productive. Stress becomes a problem only when the demands of any given situation appear to exceed our ability to cope. When the outcome seems important but the progress or conclusion is beyond or out of our control, the result is negativity, loss of perspective or, as the experts like to label it 'dystress'.

Advising people to avoid stress is, in my view, something of a waste of time in a society as rushed and hurried as ours. Learning to cope with it is, however, perfectly possible. And so is providing the body with additional protection against the devastation stress can cause.

The link with essential fatty acids

Although no-one yet knows for sure why negative stress so often leads to ill health, it *is* known that an over-production of certain hormones can lead to a weakened immunity. A body under continual stress is likely to be shooting hormones into the blood on a more or less permanent basis, leading to hyperactive adrenal glands and, eventually, adrenal exhaustion.

In addition, an absence of those very essential fatty acids which we have been reading so much about can also reduce immune strength, leaving the body more open to viral attack. (See Chapter 8 for how to stay fighting fit.) When the body is under stress, the hormones which it produces as a response not only decrease the ability of the person to resist infection but also block the conversion of fatty acids into GLA and thus helpful prostaglandins – some of which are very active fighters in the immune system force.

Action-plan for stress

Side-step stress by putting some or all of these tips into practice:

- Take regular nutritional supplements to give yourself that extra health insurance. For example, the GLA found in evening primrose oil is vital for a healthy nervous system and helps reduce the risk of infection. B vitamins can protect against stress-induced illness and give support to the nervous system, too. Vitamin C provides vital sustenance to the adrenal glands and boosts immunity. The minerals calcium and magnesium are calming and soothing – and vitamins A and E, zinc and selenium are also immune-strengthening.
- Think positively.
- Don't be always at someone else's beck and call. Take time off from your responsibility to others. Look after yourself.
- Learn to delegate. Let someone else help you out.
- Give yourself that important extra breathing space at the beginning of the day by getting up fifteen minutes earlier – now you'll have time to sit down to eat your breakfast.
- Every time you book an appointment, tell yourself that it is a quarter of an hour earlier than it really is. These few precious minutes can make the difference between arriving dishevelled, disorganized and out of breath or calm, in control and ready for action.
- Learn to say 'no'. Always being available may be more of a health hazard than you realize.
- Avoid driver stress. Don't let aggressive or irritating drivers upset you. There's really no point and it achieves nothing – except perhaps putting you at risk. And when you are considering racing ahead at the traffic lights, overtaking when it isn't safe or putting yourself at risk by rushing, ask yourself if it's really necessary.
- Be tolerant. That hesitant driver in front of you may be new to the area and trying to find his way; or perhaps a learner – which you were once.
- Don't let traffic jams turn you into an aggressive wreck. Getting angry over situations which are out of your control is a health hazard and a waste of time.

- Listen to music on your car radio or cassette deck.
- Allow plenty of time for your journey. Accept that there may be traffic lights, road works, slow vehicles and other hold-ups.
- Schedule your leisure time in advance. And take it when it comes around.
- Don't be too anxious to please. Much of the stress we put ourselves through comes from a misplaced need to be needed; to gain the approval of others.
- Take regular exercise. It's a wonderful way to release tension.
- It is said that good listeners make the best conversation. Stressed people are often 'button-holers' who never let the other person get a word in. Try to listen to what others have to say and take a genuine interest in them instead of feeling a constant need to tell *them* about *you*. Adopting this attitude will slow you down and reduce your stress levels.
- If someone upsets you (and you feel like lashing out) extract yourself from the situation as calmly and quickly as you can. When you are alone, speak your frustrations out loud, pretending that the object of your anger is standing right there in front of you. Or write them a letter and then tear it up. Sounds futile – but it works.
- When unavoidable stressful situations present themselves, ask yourself if what is happening is really going to matter in a hundred years' time – or even in a hundred minutes!
- Carry Bach Flower Rescue Remedy with you and, whenever stress strikes, squeeze a few drops under your tongue.
- Take time out to stop and stare. Admire the view, people watch, stop for a cup of tea, or read a few pages from a favourite novel or browse through a magazine article.
- Count your blessings. Make a list of everyday things which you really enjoy.
- Don't let yourself become overtired.
- Book regular aromatherapy, reflexology and/or yoga

sessions. And look upon them not as luxuries but as necessities.

- If sleep eludes you, try a herbal compound of passiflora, hops, skullcap and valerian. Hop pillows can be helpful and some people find camomile tea relaxing and calming.
- Use lavender and geranium oils in the bath water. And put a few drops on to a tissue, under your pillow.
- Eat regular meals – and spend a few minutes sitting quietly afterwards. Good nutrition and proper digestion will supply the body with many of the nutrients vital for stress protection.
- Make sure your diet contains lots of fresh salads, vegetables, fruits and wholegrains – foods which are packed with anti-stress protectors.
- Cut down on coffee and try to reduce your intake of other stimulants such as cola, alcohol, sugar, salt and cigarettes. These may be the things you turn to in a crisis but, in excess, they'll only make it harder, not easier, for the body to cope.
- Don't work through your lunch break and don't eat in the same room you work in. At home, don't pressure yourself to clear the table or wash up immediately.

Alan reports that he found these tips particularly helpful. It seems that the pressure he was under at work intensified after he began his treatment and he didn't really expect any of the recommendations to make any difference. However, he keeps in touch regularly and tells me that he feels 'a million times better'. Interestingly, he stopped taking his evening primrose oil capsules after four months ('I just forgot') but didn't feel so well without them and so has gone back to taking a regular two capsules daily.

Sources:

Newell G. R., 'Stress and cancer: the interactions of mind and body', *Primary Care In Cancer* (1991) 29–30.
Singh A., Smoak B., Patterson K. *et al.*, 'Biochemical indices of

selected trace minerals in men: effect of stress', *American Journal of Clinical Nutrition* 53 (1991) 126–31.

Horrobin D. F., 'Essential fatty acids, immunity and viral infections', *Journal of Nutritional Medicine* 1 (1990), 145–51.

Stroesser A. V., 'Effect of acute infection on iodine number of serum fatty acids', *Proc.Soc.Exp.Biol.Med.* 32 (1935), 1326–27.

Lettko M., Meuer S., 'Vitamin B-induced prevention of stress-related immunosuppression: results of a double-blind clinical study', *Ann.NY.Acad.Sci* 585 (1990), 513–15.

Driver Stress – Is it driving you round the bend? (The Health Promotion Research Trust, 49-53 Regent Street, Cambridge CB2 1AB).

Shafran S. D., *et al.*, 'Chronic Fatigue Syndrome', *Am.J.Med.* 90 (1991), 730–40.

8

Fighting fit

The discomfort of colds and flu is something that most people would choose to avoid if they could. But as soon as winter strikes doors and windows are quickly closed, the central heating goes up, and huge numbers of people go down with all manner of miserable symptoms – usually multiplied by gleeful but nasty little viruses who delight in bouncing from one innocent victim to the next. Although cold viruses are often blamed on cold weather, the actual fall in temperature is not the cause. It's this huddling together in a closed environment which makes colds and flu so much more common in winter than the summer. Once infected, people may *feel* the cold temperatures outside more easily – a natural response to a virus. Shivering (the rapid movement of muscles) helps the body to raise its core temperature; exercise would have a similar effect.

A cure for the common cold has eluded scientists because, it is always pointed out, there are so many different varieties of the virus that it has so far proved impossible to come up with a suitable vaccine. Even the experts who gather together each year to decide which bugs to put in the influenza injections don't always choose the right ones.

Viruses on the increase

All manner of viral illnesses are on the increase and new ones are being discovered and named all the time. Perhaps they have been around, sight unseen, since time immemorial and we just didn't know they were there – but for a variety of reasons, our immune systems seem less and less able to fight the wretched things off.

Stuart, a former patient of mine, would be the first to agree. He is an engineer, aged twenty-eight, lives alone, and loves junk food. In 1990 he went down with a very severe head cold. A hacking cough, chest pain, tonsillitis, ear ache, blocked sinuses, and six courses of antibiotics later and Stuart's worried sister brought him to see me. The aftermath of that cold had plagued him for a year and a half!

Stuart admitted that he felt so ill that he was ready to try anything. He took readily to my suggestion of eating more fresh fruits and vegetables and soon was in the habit of carrying fresh produce with him on the many long car journeys which were part of his job. I was pleased when he gave up his take-aways in favour of what became favourite meals of grilled trout or mackerel with salad. Jacket potatoes and stir-fries made quick-to-prepare meals when Stuart was working late.

Unfortunately, however, although he felt better for a change of diet, it was not enough to reduce the persistent infections. At the second visit, I prescribed a six-week programme of vitamin C complex (two grams daily) and six capsules of evening primrose oil – three to be taken with breakfast and three with the evening meal. After six weeks the dose was to be reduced to one gram of vitamin C complex and three capsules of evening primrose oil.

Excitingly, after only three weeks of supplements, Stuart telephoned me to say that his symptoms had gone. More than a year later, he has not suffered any illnesses at all, despite the fact that several of his work colleagues have had colds and flu throughout the winter months.

Stuart continues to take his supplements and remains symptom-free. As seems to happen so often, he did try without his evening primrose oil and vitamin C for a month in the following spring but felt 'sort of off-colour'. 'I was eating a very healthy diet,' he told me, 'but perhaps I have the kind of immune system that needs a little extra help?'

Could GLA hold the answer?

The idea that additional nutrients such as certain vitamins and the GLA found in evening primrose oil might be able to shield us against infections may seem strange, but look a little deeper and it makes good sense.

The body calls upon many different branches of its 'armed forces' to attack a virus infection. When a cold strikes, the unpleasant symptoms which you experience – such as high temperature and swollen glands – are signs that the immune system is working hard to chase and kill the invader. Specially trained forces called T-lymphocytes work undercover and are assigned to target the enemy inside the cell. A uniformed soldier, interferon, helps prevent the virus from breeding and spreading. In addition, interferon stimulates fever which, in turn, raises body temperature and encourages further anti-viral activity.

But, as with so many other bodily functions, these fighters cannot do their job without a regular supply of high quality nourishment: vitamins A, B_6, C and E; zinc, and selenium, for example, and (yes, you've guessed it) – essential fatty acids. Scientists are still trying to understand the precise role of essential fatty acids in immune function, but what they have discovered is that when there aren't enough of them the production of interferon and T-lymphocytes is impaired, making susceptibility to infections far more likely. When there are enough of them around, essential fatty acids can also be deployed for direct attacks against those viruses which try to hide and protect themselves with a lipid (fatty) envelope. Because the essential fatty acid is derived from a similar fatty substance, it is able to unlock the door to the viral cell, sneak up on the virus and destroy it.

ME and AIDS

As long ago as 1935, researchers discovered a link between essential fatty acids and infection. Fifty years later, it was found that patients suffering from AIDS had very low concentrations of essential fatty acids. So, too, do sufferers of a prolonged (and much misunderstood) condition, ME (myalgic encephalomyelitis), also known as post-viral or chronic fatigue syndrome. In a fascinating study carried out at Glasgow University, eighty-five per cent of people with ME improved when they were given a mixture of GLA and EPA (the essential fatty acid found in oily fish). In Africa, essential fatty acids have been used to help AIDS sufferers: patients reported less fatigue, a reduction in diarrhoea and improvements in skin condition. Blood tests also showed a beneficial increase in the level of virus-destroying lymphocytes.

Essential fatty acids and cancer prevention

In cancer treatment, GLA has been shown to reduce tumour size and increase survival rates. In these and other studies, the therapy proved to be extremely safe, with no adverse side effects. According to the renowned expert Dr Johanna Budwig, the proliferation of cancer cells may be closely related to problems of both oxygen and essential fatty acid deficiency.

Cancer cells do not like oxygen and, by their very nature, are oxygen-deficient. For oxygen to be transported around the body, essential fatty acids are absolutely vital. They carry this life-giving gas to the cells and remove waste carbon dioxide which is then returned to the lungs for discharge. Without essential fatty acids the flow of nutrients is disrupted and waste products and toxins (including undesirable fats) build up inside the tissues. Some experts speculate that this lack of nutrients and 'choking' of normal cell function may play some negative role in the abnormal multiplication of cancer cells. Keeping the body supplied with the right levels – and kinds – of essential fatty acids may indeed be a step in the direction of cancer prevention.

Eczema and viruses

People with atopic eczema appear to have an inherited abnormality which prevents them from converting the essential fatty acids in food to biologically-active essential fatty acids (such as GLA) and thus to all-important prostaglandins. It has also been discovered that they are far more susceptible to viral attacks such as herpes, Epstein-Barr virus, and chest infections. The reasonable conclusion has to be that their likely lack of essential fatty acids leaves them less well protected. By taking a regular supply of the missing nutrients in the usable form of supplements, eczema sufferers will hopefully cease to be an easy target for viruses.

This link between essential fatty acid deficiency and immune disorders has led to a fund of new research which confirms that a deficiency in essential fatty acids leads to a lowering of the body's defences. Whilst too few essential fatty acids can increase the likelihood of infection, a virus itself can also change essential fatty acid levels by stopping them from working within the body. The consequence is a vicious circle of an initial deficiency resulting in, say, a heavy cold or bout of influenza (both caused by viruses), which then leads to further deficiency, and a continuing spiral of persistent and recurring infections.

Action-plan for the common cold

Think twice before taking symptom-depressing medicines and cold 'remedies' if you are laid low with a slight temperature. Remember that mild fever is part of the body's active response to infection. Damping it down with para-cetamol may appear to provide a short-term improvement but will also have a detrimental effect upon the immune system's troops, encouraging them to stand down and stop fighting. In fact, the anti-viral effects of your body's interferon are greatly inhibited by many different kinds of drug medicines.

Deal with a cold speedily and swiftly by:

- Staying at home.
- Taking a hot bath.
- Going to bed immediately afterwards and remaining there for twenty-four or forty-eight hours.
- Keeping well-covered and warm.
- Drinking plenty of water, soup, herbal tea, and vegetable and fruit juices.
- Avoiding solid food.
- Taking two grams of vitamin C every four hours until symptoms subside.

Once you have recovered, introduce daily supplements of evening primrose oil and vitamin C to reduce the risk of recurrence. I have many patients who find this a most effective preventive remedy. Stuart certainly did! See Chapter 10 for recommended dosages.

Sources:

Begin M. E., Manku M. S., Horrobin D. F., 'Plasma fatty acid levels in patients with acquired immune deficiency syndrome and in controls', *Prostaglandins Leukotrienes and Essential Fatty Acids 37* (1989) 135–37.

Newell G. R., 'Stress and cancer: the interactions of mind and body', *Primary Care in Cancer* (1991) 29–30.

Van der Merwe C. F., Booyens J., Katzeff I. E., 'Oral gamma-linolenic acid in 21 patients with untreatable malignancy. An ongoing pilot open clinical trial', *Br.J.Clin.Pract.* 41 (1987), 907–15.

Horrobin D. F., 'Essential fatty acids, immunity and viral infections', *Journal of Nutritional Medicine* 1 (1990), 145–51.

Stoesser A. V., 'Effect of acute infection on iodine number of serum fatty acids', *Proc.Soc.Exp.Biol.Med.* 32 (1935), 1326–7.

Manku M. S., Horrobin D. F., Morse N. L., Wright S., Burton J. L., 'Essential fatty acids in the plasma phospholipids of patients with atopic eczema', *British Journal of Dermatology* 110 (1984), 643–8.

Shafran S. D., *et al.*, 'Chronic Fatigue Syndrome', *Am.J.Med.* 90 (1991), 730–40.

Williams L. L., Doody D. M., Horrocks L. A., 'Serum fatty acid proportions are altered during the year following acute Epstein-Barr virus infection', *Lipids* 23(10) (1988), 981–8.

Horrobin D. F., 'Essential fatty acids and the post-viral fatigue syndrome', in *Post Viral Fatigue Syndrome* by Jenkins & Mowbray (1991).

Behan P. O., Behan W. M. H., Horrobin D. F., 'Effect of high doses of essential fatty acids on the postviral fatigue syndrome', *Acta. Neurol.Scand.* 82 (1990), 209–16.

Dransfield C., 'Fats and sulphur amino acids in prevention and treatment of disease', *BioMed Newsletter* 1 (1990), 6.

9

Surprising cures

Do you struggle through the winter with frozen hands and feet? Then you'll be pleased to know that one of the many beneficial side effects reported by patients who have taken GLA is an improvement in their circulation. So successful have the results have been that I now think of GLA as a first line of treatment in many circulatory problems.

Hypothermia and heart attack

Even under normal circumstances, blood will thicken when a person is exposed to cold temperatures. Blood vessels near the skin's surface are inactivated and the amount of blood in circulation decreased – all changes designed to reduce the heat lost from the body and so cut the risk of hypothermia. Every winter, newspaper headlines make much of this killer condition which takes between 100 and 200 lives in the UK every year.

Even more devastating, however, are the estimated deaths from heart attack and stroke which are triggered by the cold, and which experts believe may be ten times that for hypothermia. There are around 4,000 more deaths each week during the winter months than in the summer; half of these are estimated to be related to circulatory disorders linked to lower temperatures. When blood thickens in response to a drop in temperature, the risk of blocked arteries increases. An inadequately heated house, prolonged periods of inactivity, waiting for a train or bus in cold weather and not wrapping up sufficiently well in warm clothing can all trigger thrombosis (blood clotting) in susceptible individuals. Even people who do not feel the cold can be more at risk from these hazards during the winter. Those over fifty are in most danger because many already have artery damage. Thickened blood flows less easily and can seize up at rough points in the artery wall, causing a blockage.

Raynaud's syndrome

Where circulation is, persistently, so poor that cold limbs turn blue or purple and the ears and nose are also badly affected, the symptoms are usually recognized as Raynaud's syndrome, discovered in 1862 by Maurice Raynaud. The nervous system triggers an involuntary spasm that constricts the blood vessels resulting in poor circulation and extremely cold hands, nose, tongue, nipples, ears and feet. Numbness and pain can be very severe indeed, and in chronic cases there is a risk of gangrene. Sadly, no satisfactory medical treatment is available for this distressing complaint which seems to affect around five to ten per cent of the population and is more common in women than men.

The actual cause remains a mystery, too. Raynaud's sufferers certainly seem to have an exaggerated or hypersensitive reaction to cold. And severity can also be linked to and aggravated by other factors such as smoking, occupational risks (keyboards, drills, repetitive hand movements), some drug medicines, and existing circulatory disorders.

Evening primrose oil really helps

No-one knows for sure why evening primrose oil works so well for Raynaud's syndrome and poor circulation but the reason may be that GLA is able to lower plasma Thromboxane levels. Thromboxane A2 causes constriction of blood vessels and encourages thickening of the blood. Under normal circumstances, these are natural repair facilities which, in the event of damage, should speed healing and prevent excessive loss of blood. Unfortunately, where thromboxanes are over-produced (or the Series 1 prostaglandins derived from GLA, which have a balancing, thinning action, are in short supply), blood becomes too sticky, veins are narrowed (by the spasm) and so the blood moves more slowly and sluggishly. The result is poor circulation.

I can recall many cases where GLA brought about a complete resolution of symptoms. One particular lady remains in the forefront of my mind. Patricia is now in her sixties and had suffered with Raynaud's syndrome for most of her adult life. As many sufferers do, she approached her GP and at various times was prescribed aspirin and other drugs in the hope that they might improve her circulation. She remembers vividly shivering her way through the blistering hot summer of 1976; people laughed because she couldn't keep warm. She wore gloves in all weathers and never went out without a scarf, hat and overcoat. And she wore fur-lined boots in the house.

After commencing treatment with evening primrose oil in August, Patricia continued taking it through the winter and found after three months that she felt much warmer and more comfortable. She has continued taking evening primrose oil (at a slightly lower dose – see Chapter 10) for the past two years and has had no recurrence of the symptoms. Her circulation now behaves completely normally.

Action-plan for poor circulation

- Introduce regular daily doses of evening primrose oil and a low dose of vitamin E (200 iu daily). After three months or so, most people report a definite improvement in circulation.
- When you are outside in very cold weather, wrap up well, wear warm clothing including gloves and a hat – and keep moving. Don't sit around or wait for long periods in a cold atmosphere.
- If you do become 'cold to the marrow', hot food and hot drinks will help to warm you. But don't choose booze.

Alcohol increases the blood flow and appears to increase temperature initially as it warms the skin's surface. Unfortunately, however, this very action reduces basic body temperature as well as your perception of how cold it is.

- Take regular exercise.
- Breathe more deeply. Move the diaphragm and abdomen – not just the upper chest area. Practised regularly, deep breathing improves the transport of oxygen and other nutrients throughout the body and enhances circulation.

Prostate problems

Walter is a market gardener and is sixty-four years old. Walter's wife, Amy, recommended that he come to see me last October because she was worried about his 'waterworks problem' – needing to pass water more often, getting up in the night, and occasional incontinence. Walter was happy to discuss these problems with me but reluctant to talk to the doctor 'because I don't know him that well'.

I persuaded Walter that it was always wise to investigate any unexplained changes in bladder or bowel habit (especially if there has been any bleeding) and so, after a little coaxing from both Amy and me, he agreed to see his GP. Following a thorough examination and referral to a consultant urologist for a second opinion, benign prostate hypertrophy was diagnosed. Walter comes from a long line of medical herbalists and was reluctant to take any drugs without trying the natural alternatives first. With the doctor's encouragement, he came back to my clinic where I prescribed a combination of evening primrose oil, fish oil and a daily zinc tablet.

Five months later, Walter's prostate problems seem to have resolved themselves completely. I discovered later that the consultant had booked Walter in for an operation 'just in case' but was so pleased with his progress that he cancelled it!

Benign prostatic hypertrophy and prostatitis are conditions which commonly affect the prostate gland, the small gland in men which is situated under the bladder and around the urethra (the first part of the urine tube). Prostate problems are extremely common in men over the age of fifty.

Benign prostate problems are not by themselves life-endangering, but if ignored they may lead to more serious difficulties; cancer being one of them. The first signs of prostate problems are usually the need to pass water during the night, the need to go more often, and pain on passing urine. Often there is the feeling of inadequate emptying both of the bladder and the bowels. Incontinence and back pain are also common symptoms. In some cases, an enlarged prostate gland may swell to the point where the outflow of urine is completely blocked, requiring emergency catheterization. If a problem is suspected, it should not be ignored. Diagnosis is confirmed by a simple blood test and examination. Inflammation may indicate a bacterial infection which, if not treated, could cause impotence.

In many cases, benign prostate hypertrophy responds well to nutritional treatment, especially to supplementation with fish oil capsules and evening primrose oil. Although drugs and/or surgery may be the only treatment suggestions made by your GP, it is always worth talking to your doctor about the possibility of using natural therapies.

All drug medicines are toxic to a greater or lesser degree and many have side effects. Surgery should be discussed in detail with your medical advisers before any decisions are finalized. Studies of patients at the Middlesex Hospital in London revealed several cases of increased heart-attack risk in those undergoing prostate operations, believed to be due to the irrigation fluids used during the operation itself. In addition, the possibility of reduced sexual function (common after surgery) also needs to be considered.

Another study has shown increased risk of prostate cancer (the second most common form in men, next to lung cancer) in men who have undergone vasectomy.

Action-plan for prostate problems

My favoured treatment for prostate difficulties consists of fish oil, evening primrose oil, multiminerals (which include zinc), amino acids, vitamin C and herbal medicines including pollen extract. Increasing dietary fibre, fresh fish, fresh fruits, vegetables and salads, cutting down on red meat, sugar, coffee, tea and alcohol, drinking more water and taking regular exercise are also important changes.

10

Dosage do's and don'ts

I have talked a great deal about the benefits of evening primrose oil throughout this book, but unfortunately not all evening primrose oil products are of the same quality. The two most reliable ways of sorting the wheat from the chaff are product labelling and price. Scan the labels and you'll see that several makes contain a range of utterly unnecessary additives. Simply choose products which contain nothing more than evening primrose oil (as the first ingredient on the list) and vitamin E (which helps prevent oxidation). Some evening primrose oil capsules also contain borage oil, another rich source of GLA, But avoid any evening primrose oil and/or borage oil products which seem particularly cheap. They are likely to contain cheap ingredients – poorly formulated and of poor quality.

The growing, monitoring, harvesting, transporting, refining and packaging of quality evening primrose oil is a costly business. Time and attention – and quality control – are vital if the product is to be of benefit. Seeds sown in the late summer are not ready for harvesting for a full fourteen months. In addition, it takes a whole acre of land to produce only 450 lbs of power-packed seeds; manufacturers need five tons of seeds to produce one ton of oil; that works out at 5,000 seeds per capsule! In my experience, cheap evening primrose oil products are simply not effective; indeed, if the oil has not been protected from oxidation by the more expensive storage, processing and encapsulation methods, it's probably already rancid and could, therefore, be a serious health hazard. I advise people to look on evening primrose oil as a real health investment.

It's worth remembering that both evening primrose oil and borage oil are recommended because of their GLA content. When deciding how much to take for any particular condition, it is the quantity of GLA per capsule that is significant. Product labels will usually tell you how much GLA there is, and most of the quality brands available will have between eight per cent and fifteen per cent per capsule. Although the pack will also give details about the amount of oil (for instance 500 mg capsules), the percentage of GLA is even more important. If labels either lack detail or give long lists of ingredients with chemical sounding names, steer clear!

Where a capsule contains eight per cent GLA, you will need to swallow twice as many as if it contains fifteen per cent. The recommendations below are worked out using fifteen per cent GLA capsules, so remember to adjust the dose accordingly if the product you have chosen contains less than this. Some of the evening primrose oil available on prescription is supplied in lower-dose capsules of eight per cent GLA, so instead of three capsules daily for eczema, your GP may suggest taking six.

In some cases, it may be recommended that you use a higher does to begin with and then reduce the number of capsules after a few months of treatment. If on cutting down you find that the condition becomes worse again, increase the dose to the original higher amount.

And please, remember that GLA is best regarded as a helpful addition to a good-quality diet. It is not a cure-all and won't benefit everyone. The wealth of anecdotal evidence amassed over many years would certainly seem to support its use as a valuable supplement for a wide range of conditions, but the only sure-fire way to corroborate the multitude of testimonials is to clamour for more and more long-term scientific research.

Does evening primrose oil have any side effects?

There have been occasional reports of slight nausea (which may occur if the oil is taken on an empty stomach), mild skin rashes or occasional acne. I have also heard of one patient who reported tingling in the limbs and slight dizziness. These side effects are extremely rare and, where they do occur, it is, of course, best to stop using the supplements. GLA and evening primrose oil are not recommended for use by epileptics or those taking strong anti-depressant or anti-psychotic drugs. If you would like to take evening primrose oil but need further information, do check with your doctor or pharmacist. The most usual side effects reported by users of evening primrose oil are the favourable ones such as stronger nails, glossier hair and fewer infections. Evening primrose oil has been studied extensively worldwide with many positive and promising findings being reported. Even where it is used in large doses, there have been no significant adverse reactions.

I feel certain that conscientious manufacturers, practitioners and consumers would welcome any regulated increase in standards so that poor quality products are either improved or removed from the market. Apart from anything else, it seems absolutely crazy to me that GLA products which are so valued for the help they seem to offer to allergic conditions like eczema are allowed to contain additives – to which so many sufferers are sensitive.

Conditions evening primrose oil can help:

- Arthritis
- Cystic fibrosis
- Diabetes – essential fatty acids may help reduce the effects of diabetic nerve damage
- Dry, dull or lifeless hair
- Dry, gritty eyes or lack of saliva
- Dry or flaking skin
- Eczema
- Excessive stress and anxiety
- Flaking or ridged fingernails
- Frequent colds and infections
- Gallbladder problems
- Hair loss – other than normal male-pattern baldness
- Heart disease
- High blood pressure
- High cholesterol
- Hyperactivity
- Infertility
- If you have recently been in hospital or are waiting for an operation. Essential fatty acids are known to be lacking in those who have suffered injury or undergone surgery, and are often lost if a patient is given glucose.
- Jumpy nerves
- Low energy levels
- Mastalgia (breast pain)
- ME (chronic or post-viral fatigue syndrome)
- Menopausal problems
- Painful or stiff joints
- Persistent tiredness
- PMS (Pre-menstrual syndrome)
- Poor circulation
- Poor wound-healing
- Raynaud's syndrome
- Rheumatism
- Sjogren's syndrome
- Vaginal dryness

**Recommended dosages
(based on 15% GLA capsules)**

Arthritis:	4 capsules daily.
Babies & children:	
up to age 5:	2 capsules daily, rubbed into the skin.
aged 6–7:	3 capsules daily, rubbed into the skin.
8 and over:	4 capsules daily, preferably swallowed.
Eczema:	3 to 6 capsules daily or as recommended by your doctor.
General protection & prevention:	1 or 2 capsules daily.
Hangover:	6 capsules with a light meal *before drinking*.
Healthy hair and nails:	1 or 2 capsules daily.
Mastalgia:	3 or 4 capsules daily or as recommended by your doctor.
ME (chronic fatigue syndrome):	4 capsules daily.
Menopause:	3 capsules daily for 3 months, reducing to one capsule daily after three months.
PMS:	3 capsules daily for 6 months, reducing to 2 capsules thereafter.
Poor circulation:	2 capsules daily.
Prostate problems:	3 capsules daily (plus fish oil supplement).
Raynaud's syndrome:	3 capsules daily from October to March; 2 capsules daily from April to September.
Sjogren's syndrome (dry eyes/lack of saliva):	3 capsules daily.

Tips and traps

- If you suffer with diabetes, ME, high cholesterol, heart diseases, rheumatoid arthritis, prostate problems or multiple sclerosis, take evening primrose oil *with* fish oil. Fish oil capsules (MaxEPA) are available on prescription for high blood pressure but may be prescribed for other conditions at the discretion of your GP. They are also available from health food stores and some chemists.
- Remember that it can take several weeks, sometimes even three or four months, for supplements to show their beneficial effects. I have met many people over the years who have dismissed evening primrose oil as 'useless' but, on investigation, I've usually found that they tried a one-capsule a day dose for only a week or two! Thinking that nothing was happening they gave up. But it's worth remembering that deficiencies can build up over very long periods of time; repair and replenishment can be a slow process but this doesn't mean your supplements aren't working.
- Once it is working and the benefits are beginning to show, don't suddenly stop taking your daily capsules. You could soon find that the original problem returns. Many chronic conditions – such as eczema, for example – are likely to require long-term or permanent evening primrose oil treatment in conjunction with sensible dietary management.
- For mastalgia (breast pain) and eczema, evening primrose oil is available on prescription. Your doctor may, at his own discretion, also be willing to prescribe evening primrose oil for other conditions, especially if you have already tried it out for yourself and found it to be helpful.
- If evening primrose oil is offered to you at a really low price, don't buy it. The very inexpensive brands are usually of extremely poor quality.

- Avoid buying evening primrose oil as a liquid. Whatever the supplier tells you, it may have been exposed to oxygen and light and will therefore have already degenerated. Further deterioration will take place each time the cap is removed, rendering the oil not only nutritionally worthless but also potentially dangerous.
- The word 'supplement' means what it says. Neither evening primrose oil, borage oil, fish oil nor any other nutrient supplement are substitutes for either a good quality diet or sensible exercise programme. No one should expect to continue to abuse their health and indulge in all the wrong kinds of foods and then expect capsules or tablets to provide an exclusive answer to their ills.
- Evening primrose oil is a very safe, non-toxic product with an excellent track record. It should not, however, be looked upon as a magic bullet or cure-all but rather as a worthwhile way to supplement the diet with those often-missing but absolutely vital and essential fatty acids.

Questions and queries

Q. *My doctor has prescribed evening primrose oil for my mastalgia. I've been taking it for three weeks but it hasn't made any difference. He tells me that it could be twelve or even sixteen weeks before things improve. Can this be right?*

A. Yes. Essential fatty acids can take several weeks or even months to make their useful presence felt. Scientists have not yet been able to work out why they take this length of time but it may be that where deficiency has been around for a long time those vital essential fatty acids have a lot of repair work to carry out. Perseverance pays, so don't give up. My patients tell me that breast pain usually begins to reduce after about three cycles.

Q. *My wife and two daughters, aged nineteen and twenty-three, swear by evening primrose oil and are trying to persuade me to take it. They tell me it could help reduce the risk of heart disease. I thought it was just for female problems but am willing to give it a try. What do you think?*

A. Evening primrose is certainly helpful in relieving a variety of female-only conditions, but it is also used for many other health problems which affect both sexes and studies do show that essential fatty acids may be protective against heart disease. Since evening primrose oil is so good for so many things including blood pressure, cholesterol and immunity, you might benefit from taking a maintenance dose of two capsules daily.

Q. *A girlfriend of mine tried a daily capsule of evening primrose oil because she has dry skin but stopped taking it after two weeks, saying that it was a waste of time. She even forgot to take it at all on some days. I have taken four capsules of evening primrose oil for my eczema for five years and wouldn't be without it. Do you think my friend was taking enough?*

A. No, I don't. One capsule per day may work as a maintenance dose if taken over a long period of time but this small amount is unlikely to have had any effect in only a fortnight. Why not suggest to your friend that she tries again, taking three capsules a day for three months and then two capsules? Regular dosage is essential.

Q. *I've heard that evening primrose oil is good for hangovers. Is this true or just an old wives' tale?*

A. It is definitely true – but it's no use taking evening primrose oil *after* the night out. Take six capsules with a light meal *before* drinking. No need to swallow evening primrose oil if you are having only one or two glasses of wine – but it will help if you are likely to be drinking more than this. However, it's worth remembering that evening primrose oil is a hangover helper only; it won't prevent the other adverse effects caused by too much alcohol, or allow you to drive a car safely!

Q. *I'm vegetarian. But capsules are made from gelatin – an animal-derivative. Are there any evening primrose oil products suitable for vegetarians?*

A. Evening primrose oil is suitable for vegetarians, but not yet available in non-gelatin capsules. You can squeeze out the contents and not use the capsule.

Q. *Every winter, I'm plagued with colds, flu and throat infections. Would evening primrose oil be of any help?*

A. Extensive studies show a definite connection between persistent viral infections and essential fatty acid deficiency. I would most definitely try evening primrose oil at four capsules daily. Begin dosage as soon as possible – don't wait until your next cold strikes!

Q. *My baby, Stephen, is fifteen months old. He is very lively during the day and sleeps very little. He seems well enough otherwise, but I'm exhausted. My health visitor thinks he may be hyperactive and says that evening primrose oil has helped other children with similar problems. But how do I give him evening primrose oil? He is obviously too young to swallow capsules.*

A. I agree with your health visitor that Stephen might benefit from evening primrose oil. Supplementing it is easy. Simply pierce open the contents of two capsules each day and massage one into his abdomen and the other to the insides of his thighs. *Never* attempt to use a liquid evening primrose oil. It also sounds to me as if you might be helped by a regular dose of evening primrose oil, but in capsule form. Patients do report improved energy levels, fewer infections, and a feeling of enhanced well-being.

Q. *I have read that evening primrose oil is helpful for pre-menstrual syndrome. Would it also help menopausal symptoms? I would like to try it because I can't take hormone replacement therapy.*

A. In my experience with patients, evening primrose oil – together with other nutrients such as vitamin B complex, vitamin E and magnesium – can be extremely helpful in treating and relieving the miseries of the menopause. Try three capsules a day for three months and, if you feel better, reduce the dose to one or two capsules.

Q. *My father, aged seventy-one, has recently been in hospital for a major operation and has been fed by something called a TPN for nearly six weeks. His skin has become sore, dry and flaky, his scalp is covered in dandruff and he is experiencing joint pain and stiffness. Do you think that he may be deficient in something and would evening primrose oil help him?*

A. TPN stands for total parenteral nutrition which means that your father has been receiving the nourishment he needs from drip feeding. Studies are being carried out into the long-term effects of TPN and initial results are both interesting and helpful. Unfortunately, it would appear that intravenous feeding does not always supply the right levels of fatty acids. Low levels of essential fatty acids are common in people who have undergone surgery and, particularly, in those who are fed with glucose and TPN drips. I would recommend that you voice your concerns both to your father's GP and his hospital consultant or registrar, and suggest that evening primrose oil and vitamins and minerals be used. You may like to refer the doctors to an interesting study on this subject carried out in Seattle in 1975 by Dr M. C. Riella and his colleagues. The results were reported in a publication called the *Annals of Internal Medicine* and entitled 'Essential Fatty Acid Deficiency in Human Adults During Total Parenteral Nutrition' (issue 83, 1975, pp. 786–9).

Glossary

Acid mantle – the natural, slightly acid, state of the skin which provides protection against bacteria.

Achlorhydria – Diminished supply of hydrochloric acid in the stomach.

Adrenal glands – Two tiny endocrine glands which are situated one on top of each kidney.

Adrenalin – a hormone (also known as epinephrine) which is excreted from the middle section (the medulla) of the adrenal glands.

Aldosterone – A hormone which is released by the adrenal glands and acts on the kidneys to regulate salt and water balance in the body.

Alpha-linolenic acid – A polyunsaturated fatty acid belonging to the Omega 3 family.

Amino acids – Organic molecules which are the building blocks of protein.

Antioxidants – Vitamins, minerals and enzymes which prevent the damage to and degeneration (oxidation) of tissues and cells. Antioxidants also occur naturally in susceptible food substances such as fats and oils. Vitamins A, C, B_6, E, zinc and selenium are all antioxidants.

Basal cells – Skin cells at the base of the epidermis.

Benign prostatic hypertrophy – Enlargement of the prostate gland.

Bile – The bitter, yellow-green substance produced by the liver (and stored in the gallbladder) which emulsifies fats and oils, enabling them to be digested and absorbed. Bile also neutralizes the acid semi-liquids (chyme) from the stomach as they pass into the small intestine.

Biliary colic – The pain associated with gallstones and gallbladder disease.

Bioflavonoids – Water soluble vitamin-like substance (also referred to as citrus salts or vitamin P complex). Found in most foods which contain vitamin C but particularly rich in the pith and skin of citrus fruits, in green peppers, buckwheat, beetroot, bilberries, blackberries, black cherries and gingko biloba.

Calcitonin – A hormone produced by the thyroid gland which, by inhibiting the release of calcium from the bone, reduces levels of calcium in the blood when they become too high.

Calorie – A calorie is a unit of heat, being the amount of energy required to raise the temperature of one gram of water by one degree centigrade. When written with a capital 'C', is the abbreviated version of kilocalorie so that, in most discussions about the calorific value of foods – and for all practical purposes – calorie actually means kilocalorie. For example, a 2,000-calorie-a-day diet means in fact 2,000 kilocalories.

Carcinogenic – Cancer-forming.

Cardiac arrest – Heart attack.

CHD – Coronary heart disease.

Cholesterol – A fatty substance produced by the liver, necessary for a healthy nervous system, for promoting vitamin D synthesis, and in the production of hormones. Cholesterol is also found in some foods but this is not now believed to have any detrimental effect upon the levels of cholesterol in blood. The major components of blood cholesterol are high density lipoproteins (HDL), low density lipoproteins (LDL) and very low density lipoproteins (VLDL).

Cis-fatty acids – The nutritional and biologically-active fatty acid substances found in unadulterated, unprocessed food oils. Chemically, a cis-fatty acid has all its hydrogen atoms on the same side of the chain, allowing it to bend.

Coagulate – To thicken.

Cold Pressing – A natural method of extracting oil from food substances which does not involve heat or solvents.

Collagen – A protein substance found in connective tissue. Often likened to an intercellular glue or cement because of its ability to 'hold' skin together, giving firmness and structure.

Cortisol – The body's natural cortisone, produced by the adrenal cortex in response to stress. Involved in blood glucose balance and also has anti-inflammatory and pain control properties.

DHA (docosahexaenoic acid) – One of the essential fatty acids found in fish oil. A member of the Omega 3 family and derived from alpha-linolenic acid.

Delta-6-desaturase (D-6-d) – An enzyme needed to convert the linoleic acid in food to gamma linolenic acid (GLA).

Dermis – Also called the corium, the living skin underneath the outer skin's surface.

DGLA (Dihomo gamma linolenic acid) – A polyunsaturated fatty acid which belongs to the Omega 6 family; made in the body from linoleic acid and GLA.

Elastin – A protein substance which gives the skin its elasticity.

Endocrine system – The glandular system which secretes the body's hormones such as insulin from the pancreas, oestrogen from the ovaries, and adrenalin from the adrenal glands.

Enzyme – An organic compound which acts as a bio-catalyst able to trigger a series of activities within the body without its own structure being altered.

EPA (eicosapentaenoic acid) – An essential fatty acid found in oily fish. A member of the Omega 3 family, derived from alpha-linolenic acid.

Epidermis – The upper outer layer of surface skin cells.

Erucic acid – A fatty acid belonging to the Omega 9 family and the principal fatty acid of rapeseed oil. Can be toxic if ingested in large quantities. New genetically engineered varieties of rapeseed oil are said to contain only two per cent erucic acid but, to the best of my knowledge and extensive research, no long-term studies have been carried out to test for safety at these levels.

Essential fatty acids – Vital nutrients which cannot be manufactured by the body and so must be provided from diet. An important energy source, they are also needed to provide cell structure and to produce prostaglandins.

Familial hypercholesterolaemia – Inherited high cholesterol.

Fibrinogen – A substance in the blood which allows it to clot when necessary.

Free radicals – Unstable, highly reactive molecules which damage polyunsaturated fatty acids and can lead to cell destruction.

Gallstones – Concretions (usually made of hardened cholesterol deposits) which form in gallbladder and/or bile duct.

Follicle-stimulating hormone (FSH) – A hormone which is released by the pituitary gland and stimulates ovulation.

GLA (gamma linolenic acid) – A polyunsaturated fatty acid belonging to the Omega 6 family. In the presence of the correct enzyme (delta-6-desaturase), GLA can be derived from linoleic acid in the body. GLA itself is not commonly found in the normal diet, borage seed, blackcurrant seed and evening primrose seed being the best known sources. Also found in breast milk.

High density lipoproteins (HDL) – *See* Cholesterol.

Hormone – A secretion from an endocrine gland in the body which acts as a messenger to another part of the body.

Hydrogenation – A manufacturing process which turns liquid oils into solid fats and, in so doing, makes some of the polyunsaturates into saturates and cis-fatty acids into trans-fatty acids.

Hypercholesterolaemia *See* Familial hypercholesterolaemia.

Hyperglycaemia – Elevated blood sugar.

Hyperventilation – Abnormal and rapid over-breathing.

Hypochlorhydria – Low levels of hydrochloric acid in the stomach.

Hypoglycaemia – Low blood sugar.

Hypertension – High blood pressure.

Hypotension – Low blood pressure.

Interferon – A family of proteins which are employed by the immune system to work inside cells and fight viruses. Interferon has a known anti-cancer effect.

Keratin – The tough protein constituent of hair, skin and nails.

Kilocalorie – One thousand calories; *See* Calorie.

Lecithin – Accurately means the phospholipid substance known as phosphatidylcholine. However, the food industry uses a lecithin compound which includes vegetable oils and fatty acids; an emulsifying agent, being partly soluble in both fats and water. The natural emulsifier in egg yolk is lecithin.

Lipid – The biochemical term for fatty acids and fatty substances.

Lipid peroxidation – Describes the harmful oxidation of fats and oils which can trigger free radical damage. Fat in food which has suffered from peroxidation is rancid and may have a strong and unpleasant taste and/or odour.

Low density lipoproteins (LDL) – *See* Cholesterol.

Melanin – The brown pigment, produced from the amino acid tyrosine, found in skin. Its level of concentration will determine the depth of skin colour.

Monounsaturates – Oils found in such foods as avocado pear, some nuts and in olive oil. Monunsaturated fatty acids are those which contain only one double bond. (Saturates have no double bonds and polyunsaturates have two or more). Monounsaturates are liquid at room temperature but will solidify if refrigerated. They are more stable than polyunsaturates and therefore suitable for cooking.

Multiple sclerosis – Inflammation and hardening of parts of the central nervous system with consequent damage to the myelin sheath which protects nerves in the brain and spinal cord. A widespread, progressive disease which varies in intensity and is characterized by periods of exacerbation and remission.

Noradrenalin – Also called norepinephrine. A hormone messenger produced by the adrenal medulla.

Oestrogen – A female hormone produced by the ovaries and, in smaller amounts, by healthy adrenal glands.

Oxidation – Damage caused by oxygen attack, as in rusting iron, perishing rubber or browning apples. In the body, oxidation is a natural process which triggers the release of energy from foodstuffs. However, in excess, it can lead to cell damage and premature ageing.

Parathyroid hormone – A hormone produced by the parathyroid glands and responsible for (with the hormone calcitonin) regulating calcium levels in the blood. When calcium levels fall, parathyroid hormone triggers the release of calcium from the bones.

Peak bone mass – A term used to refer to the age when bone growth finishes (usually between the ages of thirty and forty).

Phosphatidylcholine – A phospholipid – also referred to as lecithin. An important structural component of cell membranes and lipoproteins. Also a precursor to the neurotransmitter (nerve messenger) acetylcholine.

Pituitary gland – Known as the master gland, the 'conductor' of the endocrine system and of all hormones. It is situated in the brain.

Polyunsaturates – Oils found in foods predominantly of vegetable origin (and also in fish) which remain liquid once extracted. **Polyunsaturated fatty acids (PUFAs)** are those with two or more double bonds.

Progesterone – A female hormone secreted in the latter half of the ovarian cycle.

Prolactin – A hormone produced by the anterior pituitary gland which stimulates the mammary glands to produce breast milk.

Prostaglandins – Biologically active local messengers derived from essential fatty acids which regulate a variety of body functions. They fall into three categories or series and each has a different chemical structure:

Series 1 – Originate from linoleic acid and GLA.

Series 2 – Also originate from linoleic acid, but in addition can be absorbed directly (and in excess) from meat, milk, and related products.

Series 3 – Originate from alpha-linolenic acid and EPA.

Prostatis – Inflammation of the prostate gland, usually due to infection.

Prostate gland – A gland in men which lies at the base of the bladder and is responsible for secretions which maintain sperm activity.

Saturates – Fats found predominantly in foods of animal origin and which are solid at room temperature, such as lard, butter, and dripping. Saturated fatty acids have only single bonds.

Sebaceous gland – The oil-secreting glands of the scalp and skin.

Sebum – The oil produced by the sebaceous glands.

Sensory receptors – Nerve fibres which relay information from the sense organs to the brain.

Serotonin – A neurotransmitter (nerve messenger) and vasoconstrictor (prevents bleeding by tightening blood vessels) which is derived from the amino acid tryptophan. Serotonin is also active in the brain, regulating mood and assisting sleep.

Serum – The clear fluid which is left over after blood has clotted.

T-lymphocyte – Produced from thymosin (a hormone secreted by the thymus gland). T-lymphocytes work inside cells helping to attack viruses.

Thromboxanes – Blood clotting agents produced by Series 2 prostaglandins.

Trans-fatty acids – Produced when cis-fatty acids are detrimentally altered, usually by food processing methods. The natural configuration of essential fatty acids is damaged and the fatty acids are no longer nutritionally active. *See* p. 40.

Triglycerides – Molecules of oil or fat.

Very low density lipoproteins – *See* Cholesterol.

Index